A CONCISE GUIDE TO IMPROVING

STUDENT LEARNING

A gift from

THE FACULTY CENTER
for
TEACHING AND LEARNING
AUSTIN COMMUNITY COLLEGE

A CONCISE GUIDE TO IMPROVING STUDENT LEARNING

Six Evidence-Based Principles and How to Apply Them

Diane Cummings Persellin and Mary Blythe Daniels

Foreword by Michael Reder

STERLING, VIRGINIA

Published by Stylus Publishing, LLC
22883 Quicksilver Drive
Sterling, Virginia 20166-2102

Library of Congress Cataloging-in-Publication Data

Persellin, Diane.
A concise guide to improving student learning : six evidence-based
principles and how to apply them / Diane Cummings Persellin and
Mary Blythe Daniels.—First Edition.
    pages cm
Includes bibliographical references and index.
ISBN 978-1-62036-091-0 (cloth : alk. paper)—
ISBN 978-1-62036-092-7 (pbk. : alk. paper)—
ISBN 978-1-62036-093-4 (library networkable e-edition)—
ISBN 978-1-62036-094-1 (consumer e-edition)
1. College teaching—Handbooks, manuals, etc.
I. Daniels, Mary Blythe. II. Title.

LB2331.P425 2014
378.1'25—dc23
                                                    2013049706

13-digit ISBN: 978-1-62036-091-0 (cloth)
13-digit ISBN: 978-1-62036-092-7 (paperback)
13-digit ISBN: 978-1-62036-093-4 (library networkable e-edition)
13-digit ISBN: 978-1-62036-094-1 (consumer e-edition)

Printed in the United States of America

All first editions printed on acid-free paper
that meets the American National Standards Institute
Z39-48 Standard.

Bulk Purchases

Quantity discounts are available for use in workshops and for
staff development.
Call 1-800-232-0223

First Edition, 2014

10   9   8   7   6

To my parents, Floyce and Kent Cummings; my favorite teacher,
Carole Flatau; and my husband, Robert Persellin,
for their inspiration and encouragement.
DCP

For my mother, Rachel Daniels, who inspired me to teach.
In memory of my brother-in-law, Patrick Mulholland,
who inspired so many to learn.
MBD

CONTENTS

FOREWORD

Brevity is the soul of wit.

—*Hamlet*, William Shakespeare

You have in your hand, in one compact package, a primer, a detailed guidebook to becoming a more effective teacher. In just 60 pages of main text you will find rich morsels, insights, and wisdom about approaches to improving student learning. Professors Persellin and Daniels have combed through the best ideas about effective teaching and learning, straining them down to six straightforward principles. The most recent literature on how learning works—such as James Zull on the neuropsychology of learning, Susan Ambrose and colleagues on research-based teaching, Dee Fink on course design—shape these principles. The authors also take into account contemporary theories of student intellectual development, as well as the current larger conversations taking place about higher education. It will aid you in making educated, intentional decisions about your teaching and course design—decisions based not only on hunches or feelings or previous experiences, but on research and theory.

Informed by research, the approaches and examples in this book are real-world, rooted not just in theory but also in practice. Each of the six principles has clear instructional applications, and is illustrated by a series of brief suggestions for assignments or techniques, enabling you to easily apply these ideas to your own courses and teaching. Following each principle, the authors include a short annotated bibliography of the research studies that inform these practices, allowing you to delve deeper into the literature.

The book also includes a series of written workshops on best practices, offering more in-depth examinations of key approaches to improving student learning. Rich in examples and resources, these workshops both offer insights into some of the most powerful curricular learning experiences—such as writing and community learning—as well as elaborate on more specific, classroom-based teaching techniques—such as how to develop and use rubrics, approach formative assessment and foster student self-reflection, and offer effective feedback on essays and exams.

Like good teaching, the book is constructed to actively engage the learner. This brief but powerful work does not lecture you; *it invites you to learn*. It provides opportunities for readers to engage with these ideas and approaches and then to reflect upon them. It asks you to stop and think about your own practices, your own teaching.

Toward an Intentional, Critically Self-Reflective Practice

There is an assortment of effective approaches to teaching, and how a faculty member constructs her or his course and runs her or his classroom (or lab or studio) should accurately reflect both the variety of disciplinary styles and the individual personality and identity of that teacher. There is no single "right" or effective way to teach. This book not only acknowledges the diversity of approaches to improving student learning, but also reveals a wide range of options that allow us to make those informed choices about our teaching practices.

Whether you are an experienced teacher or a relative neophyte, the information in *A Concise Guide to Improving Student Learning* will allow you to become a more knowledgeable practitioner and approach your teaching—as we do our disciplinary scholarship and creative work—in an informed, critically reflective manner.

Why Another Book About Effective Teaching and Learning?

When I first learned about *A Concise Guide to Improving Student Learning*, the question that first came to my mind was, Why? What does this book do that is different from the other books about teaching and learning? What does this work contribute to the already substantial body of research and theory about learning, of works that address approaches to and techniques for teaching?

Those of us who have ventured into the literature on teaching and learning know that, over the past two decades, it has become a discipline unto itself. The options and resources for improving one's teaching sometimes feel limitless and overwhelming, especially for faculty members who are busily engaged not only in teaching and service, but also in research and creative work. So even though this book is focused on improving student learning, it is written by and for faculty—it is written for us. The authors are well aware of their audience, all of whom live very busy professional lives.

As a director of a faculty center for teaching and learning, a large part of my work is to take the myriad ideas about teaching and learning, separate the wheat from the chaff, and share those ideas with my colleagues. *A Concise Guide to Improving Student Learning* reviews, condenses, and explains those theories and practices—allowing you, the reader, to efficiently and effectively engage with those ideas.

Michael Reder
Director
Joy Shechtman Mankoff Center for Teaching & Learning
Connecticut College

PREFACE

This concise guidebook was designed to be a resource for academics who are interested in engaging students according to the findings of peer-reviewed literature and best practices but who do not have the time to immerse themselves in the scholarship of teaching and learning. In the last decade alone, many research studies about the process of learning have emerged at the K–12 level. Such scholarship has great potential to dramatically affect teaching. Although it seems obvious that an understanding of how learning works could transform our teaching, in higher education we have been slower to engage with this growing body of scholarship. Our book, intentionally brief, is intended to (a) summarize recent research on six of the most compelling principles in learning and teaching, (b) provide applications to the college classroom based on this research, (c) include special sections about teaching strategies that are based on best practices, and (d) offer annotated bibliographies and important citations for faculty who want to pursue additional study.

The field of teaching and learning is developing rapidly, and we have endeavored to keep up with the newly emerging body of scholarship. Many excellent books are available, and we have included recent leading research as well as seminal texts in the field. We based our six principles on research studies, most of which have been replicated in multiple settings. The six principles were chosen because, in our judgment, they are the most solidly grounded in evidence-based scholarship. Annotated bibliographies of research studies are included in the chapters as examples that illustrate the principles. The bibliography at the end of the book is broader and also includes articles and resources for teaching that are not necessarily based on research.

In the sections devoted to teaching applications, we have included a diverse range of disciplines, including sciences, humanities, arts, and pre-professional programs. Most of these applications can be implemented without extensive preparation. We encourage instructors to adapt these strategies according to specific needs, interests, disciplines, and classroom contexts.

Although the book emphasizes research-based learning, we as practitioners appreciate the need for pragmatic pedagogies. For that reason we have also included special sections dedicated to best practices, rather than research-based principles. The workshops, shaded in gray, elucidate topics such as problem-based learning, assessment strategies, concept mapping, and community-based learning.

The introduction, "Knowing About Learning Informs Our Teaching," provides an overview of how we learn that includes important topics such as the definition of *expert* and *novice learners*, memory, prior learning, and metacognition. The body of the book is divided into three chapters, each of which includes teaching principles, applications, and related strategies.

Chapter 1, "Deeper Learning and Better Retention," is divided into three research-based principles: Desirable Difficulties Increase Long-Term Retention, Meaningful and Spaced Repetition Increases Retention, and Emotion and Relevance Deepen Learning.

Chapter 2, "Actively Engaged Learning," synthesizes recent studies documenting that students who are actively engaged in meaningful and challenging activities learn more deeply. The two research-based principles presented in this chapter are Multisensory Instruction Deepens Learning and Small Groups Engage Students.

Chapter 3, "Assessment," presents one research principle: Formative Assessment or Low-Stakes Evaluation Strengthens Retention. This chapter focuses on how good assessment techniques ask students to review, apply, analyze, and evaluate current and prior learning. We also include a section on assessment resources, such as rubrics and grading strategies. The appendices address aspects of course design such as creating a syllabus, presenting a successful lecture, and leading a meaningful in-class discussion.

Owing to the scope of this book, these sections are necessarily short; we have not delved into the complexities of how each of these principles is interrelated. However, we have cross-referenced as much as possible, and we hope that the bibliographies and other resources provided will guide the interested reader to a fuller understanding of each principle. Finally, we, of course, realize not every principle or strategy in the book is suitable for everyone. Moreover, there is no one teaching strategy that will provide the silver bullet for student engagement. Our goal is to provide a foundation that will assist instructors in making good choices for their pedagogical needs.

ACKNOWLEDGMENTS

We thank the Associated Colleges of the South (ACS) Faculty Renewal Grant for supporting us in writing the pilot version of this book (Persellin & Daniels, 2012), which was distributed in celebration of the 20th anniversary of the ACS Teaching and Learning Workshop. We also are indebted to an ACS Mellon Grant for helping us substantially revise the manuscript for publication. Many people have helped us on this journey: early readers of the manuscript, Sarah Goodrum (University of Colorado, Boulder), Barbara Lom (Davidson College), Barbara MacAlpine (Trinity University), and Elizabeth Osland (Monte Esperança, Lisbon, Portugal); focus groups at Trinity University and Centre College; and the ACS Teaching and Learning Workshop staff. We appreciate the time and energy of Kent Anderson (Birmingham-Southern College), Sean Connin (Trinity University), Emily Gravett (Trinity University), Sarah Lashley (Centre College), and Harry Wallace (Trinity University), who read and commented on our final draft. A very special thanks to Robert Persellin and Laurie Davison for their support and encouragement during the writing of this book.

INTRODUCTION

Knowing About Learning Informs Our Teaching

*I never try to teach my pupils anything,
I only try to create an environment in
which they can learn.*

—Albert Einstein

*Expert learners consider the knowledge explicitly and
separate from the present task. There is consideration
for when and where that knowledge can be used
in the future. They negotiate meaning with their
peers. They ask questions. They seek
answers and construct solutions.*

—Peter Skillen (n.d.)

How can we as educators help our students remember and process information for long-term memory rather than short-term responses on an exam? How do we help students transfer their newly acquired knowledge and skills to other contexts and problems? How can we support students who are still working as novices in our more complex disciplines? In other words, how do we help our students learn? As instructors, we need to remember that our students do not think like we do, and we need to help them develop as learners.

When instructors have an understanding of the cognitive development of their students, they may be able to plan their teaching strategies more effectively. In this introduction we present a brief summary of a model for understanding student learning that contrasts novice and expert learners. To help students move along the continuum from novice to expert learners, it is important for instructors to have a framework of how memory works as well as an understanding of the importance of prior knowledge and metacognitive skills. Our intention is to provide an introduction to these topics rather

1

than a comprehensive study of neuroscience or intellectual development, which is beyond the scope of this project. For more thorough discussions and resources related to learning and cognitive development, we refer the reader to the bibliography on page 79.

Expert and Novice Learners

Students who are new to our subject areas or lack a background in the topic think differently from students who have more experience when solving problems and learning new material. Understanding the differences between how novices in our fields think about new problems and how students who have more expertise approach them can help us teach better. Bransford, Brown, and Cocking's (2000) model of expert and novice learners, even in its most basic form as presented here, is an excellent means to help instructors think about both the challenges of developing expertise and its implications for teaching. The following list of differences between expert and novice learners was adapted from Vanderbilt University (n.d.):

1. The expert learner is able to establish meaningful patterns and organize information around content, whereas novices do not necessarily recognize these patterns.
2. Experts are fluent at retrieving information, whereas novices have to apply significant effort to retrieve information. An expert's knowledge is organized to support understanding, not just memorization.
3. Experts' knowledge is not a list of isolated facts. Their knowledge is organized around broader concepts that guide their thinking. Experts frame their knowledge within a context.
4. There are both routine experts and adaptive experts. Routine experts function well in one setting but encounter difficulty in a different setting. Adaptive experts, owing to their metacognitive skills, are able to transfer knowledge to different circumstances.

Ironically, our expertise as instructors can pose pedagogical challenges when we assume our students have our level of fluency in organizing and interpreting information. It is, therefore, important for instructors to make explicit the strategies for moving from a novice learner to an independent and sophisticated thinker. That is, instructors must help students learn both to organize and integrate new information and to think critically about their own thought processes.

Memory

A widely respected theory of how memory works was first proposed by Atkinson and Shiffrin in 1968. Their model proposes that memory consists of three separate and distinct storage systems: sensory memory, short-term memory, and long-term memory. For this reason the model is called the multistore model. According to the model, new information is received by our senses. If a student is paying attention to the input, this information is quickly converted into a type of code that is stored in a working memory. Working memory, however, has a fast turnover (up to 15 seconds) and limited capacity for new information (Baddeley, 1986). Information is more likely to move from working memory to long-term memory if it is relevant to the learner, who can then place the material into a framework developed by prior knowledge. This new information is then available to be located and retrieved when needed; however, it is more easily retrieved if the information has been reinforced. Strategies that cognitive neuroscientists and other experts (Braun & Bock, 2007; Caine, Caine, McClintic, & Klimek, 2005; Kember, Ho, & Hong, 2008) have identified as being critical to committing information to long-term memory include the following:

1. *Repeating and rehearsing new information.* An entire section of this book is devoted to this important topic (see Principle 2: Meaningful and Spaced Repetition Increases Retention, p. 12). Instructors can aid students with the process of remembering by showing them connections between new information and what they already know to help make the material relevant.
2. *Establishing meaningful patterns to organize learning.* People tend to remember patterns and meaning before remembering specific details (Medina, 2008).
3. *Allowing students time to process information.* Processing is a critical component to integrating new information into long-term memory structures.
4. *Finding relevance in the learning* (see Principle 3: Emotion and Relevance Deepen Learning, p. 15). When a new topic is relevant to learners, they are better able to anchor it in their long-term memory.

A novice learner often remembers less information than an expert learner because retention is closely linked to the relationship between the new material one is learning and material one already knows. Prior knowledge is central to a learner's capacity to make meaning from new information. Students come to our courses with beliefs and attitudes gained in other courses and through daily life. Using this knowledge, students filter and interpret what they are learning. If what they already know is factually accurate, it provides a strong foundation for the construction of knowledge. However, when prior knowledge leads to misconceptions, the latter can be remarkably resistant to correction. A professor can activate prior knowledge and pave the way for new learning by asking students to make connections and to see patterns between new information and information they already know (Squire, 2004; Zull, 2002). This also allows instructors to gauge students' understanding and correct inaccurate perceptions. A teacher can then help students determine when it is appropriate to apply prior knowledge and when it is not.

Metacognition is an important part of cognitive theory and is defined as "the process of reflecting on and directing one's own thinking" (National Research Council, 2001, p. 78). In other words, students must be able both to monitor their own process and to adapt their strategies as needed (Ambrose, Bridges, DiPietro, Lovett, & Norman, 2010). To fully develop as expert learners, students must be self-aware, be responsible, and take initiative. Instructors can help students develop these traits by explicitly asking students to evaluate their own skills, encouraging them to predict outcomes, and helping them learn from their successes and failures. When students analyze how they think, deeper learning can take place (Chin & Brown, 2000). As William Perry (1970) explained, when students move from a black-and-white level of dualism as first-year students to a more discerning relativist perspective as they mature and gain more expertise and comfort with multiple perspectives, they then start to understand that most knowledge is dependent upon context. Increasingly, instructors can encourage students to think independently and analytically and to begin to view the instructor as a facilitator in the process of learning (Moore, 1989).

I

DEEPER LEARNING AND BETTER RETENTION

Great teachers [are] those people with considerable success in fostering deep approaches and results among their students.
—Ken Bain and James Zimmerman (2009)

Deep learning involves the critical analysis of new ideas, linking them to already known concepts and principles so that this understanding can be used for problem solving in new, unfamiliar contexts.
—Julian Hermida (n.d.)

Chapter 1 examines three research-based principles for teaching and learning: (a) desirable difficulties, or requiring students to work harder in the initial learning period; (b) repetition; and (c) emotion in teaching and learning. In each section we share teaching applications. The workshops, or best practices, shaded in gray address concept maps and community-based learning (CBL).

Principle 1: Desirable Difficulties Increase Long-Term Retention

We often seek to eliminate difficulties in learning, to our own detriment.
—Jeff Bye (2011)

According to the pain is the gain.
—Ben Hei Hei, *Ethics of the Fathers*, 5:21 (220 CE)

Requiring students to organize new information and to work harder in the initial learning period can lead to greater and deeper learning. Although this struggle, dubbed a *desirable difficulty* by investigator R. A. Bjork (1994), may at first be frustrating to learner and teacher alike, ultimately it improves long-term retention. For example, the research of Rohrer and Taylor (2007) revealed that increased challenges during a math class produced better long-term performance. The authors instructed subjects how to find the volume of four geometric figures. Group 1 was taught how to find the volume of only one figure, while group 2 was taught several different types of problems. Although initially the second group performed worse in practice sessions, after a week delay they outperformed the first group on tests, answering 63% of the questions correctly compared to only a 20% correct response rate from group 1.

In the short term, conditions that make learning more challenging—such as generating words instead of passively reading them, varying conditions of practice, transferring knowledge to new situations, or learning to solve multiple types of math problems at once—might slow down performance. However, there is a yield in long-term retention. At first the learner may make more errors or forget an important process,

> but it is this forgetting that actually benefits the learner in the long term; relearning forgotten material takes demonstrably less time with each iteration. The subjective difficulty of processing disfluent information can actually lead learners to engage in deeper processing strategies, which then results in higher recall for those items. (Bye, 2011)

By forcing the brain to create multiple retrieval paths, a desirable difficulty makes the information more accessible. If we can use information in multiple ways and multiple contexts, we build many pathways to memory; thus, if one pathway is blocked, we can use another.

These difficulties invite "a deeper processing of material than people would normally engage in without explicit instruction to do so" (Bjork, 1994). However, teaching with desirable difficulties can be challenging. Learners, of course, are gratified when they feel that they are processing information easily. Instructors understandably want learning to come quickly for students and may choose the method that produces immediate results. However, as Bye (2011) states, when "instructors facilitate learning by making it easier, it may increase short-term performance, but it may decrease long-term retention." Bjork (2013) suggests that once instructors decide what they want students to remember a year after their course is over, they then think about how to implement desirable difficulties into their course. This may mean introducing an important concept multiple times in different ways throughout the semester, making the important class concepts relevant to other course material (see Principle 3: Emotion and Relevance Deepen Learning, p. 15), and asking students to analyze and produce knowledge, rather than listen to the instructor present it (see chapter 2, "Actively Engaged Learning," p. 23).

Instructional Applications

Quiz Students
Quiz students on material rather than having them simply restudy or reread it (Karpicke & Blunt, 2011; Roediger & Karpicke, 2006). Even if quizzes are low-stakes assessments, they force students to generate information rather than passively read (see Principle 6: Formative Assessment or Low-Stakes Evaluation Strengthens Retention, p. 43).

Generate Knowledge
Ask learners to generate target material through an active, creative process, rather than simply by reading passively. This could involve role playing, structured debates, puzzles, or scientific study (McDaniel & Butler, 2010; see chapter 2, "Actively Engaged Learning," p. 23).

Space Practice Sessions
Have students rehearse or practice important skills during different sessions. Dempster and Farris (1990) and Cepeda, Pashler, Vul, Wixted, and Rohrer (2006) found that when sessions were spaced further apart, students were more likely to retain material (see Principle 2: Meaningful and Spaced Repetition Increases Retention, p. 12).

Allow for Confusion
When a concept is difficult, allow students to experience and work their way through their frustration. When students are able to resolve their initial confusion themselves, deeper learning takes place.

Challenge the Reader
When learners perceive that material is more difficult to read, they tend to read it with more care and process it more deeply (McNamara, Kintsch, Songer, & Kintsch, 1996). Studies suggest that even using fonts that are slightly more difficult to read affects engagement and processing (Alter, Oppenheimer, Epley, & Eyre, 2007; Diemand-Yauman, Oppenheimer, & Vaughan, 2011; Yue, Castel, & Bjork, 2013).

Wait for an Answer

Allowing time to think between asking a question and requiring an answer gives students the opportunity to better formulate their answers and, therefore, increases the depth of answers. It also lets students know the instructor will not be answering his or her own questions.

Interleave Material

Teach several skills or concepts in the same class rather than focusing on only one specific idea.

Create Concept Maps

Ask students to create a concept map. This requires them to generate relationships based on the class discussions or readings (see Workshop 1.1: Concept Maps).

Annotated Research Studies

Dempster, F., & Farris, R. (1990). The spacing effect: Research and practice. *Journal of Research and Development in Education, 23*(2), 97–101.

In this study investigators found that spaced instruction yielded significantly better learning than massed presentations. Two spaced presentations were nearly twice as effective as two massed presentations. In many cases effectiveness increased as the frequency of the presentations increased.

Diemand-Yauman, C., Oppenheimer, D., & Vaughan, E. (2011). Fortune favors the bold (and the italicized): Effects of disfluency on educational outcomes. *Cognition, 118*(1), 111–115. doi:10.1016/j.cognition.2010.09.012

This article reports the results of two studies examining the impact on learning of a font that is slightly more difficult to read. Both studies found that information in harder-to-read fonts was better remembered than information shared in easier-to-read fonts. The struggle to read the material was thought to contribute to deeper processing.

Karpicke, J., & Blunt, J. (2011). Retrieval practice produces more learning than elaborative studying with concept mapping. *Science, 331*(6018), 772–775. doi:10.1126/science.1199327

Two hundred college students were divided into four groups and asked to read several paragraphs about a scientific topic. Each group performed one of the following learning strategies: (a) reading the text for 5 minutes, (b) reading the text in four consecutive 5-minute sessions, (c) drawing diagrams about information from the excerpt they were reading, and (d) reading the passage once and taking a "retrieval practice test" that required them to write down what they recalled. A week later all four groups took a quiz asking them to recall facts from the passage they had read and to draw conclusions on the basis of those facts. The students in the fourth group, who took the practice test, recalled 50% more of the material than those in the other three groups. The investigators concluded that by organizing and creating meaningful connections, struggling to remember information, and identifying areas of weakness, students were able to better recall information.

McDaniel, M., Hines, R., Waddill, P., & Einstein, G. (1994). What makes folk tales unique: Content familiarity, causal structure, scripts, or superstructures? *Journal of Experimental Psychology: Learning, Memory, and Cognition, 20*(1), 169–184.

Investigators asked students to generate new material by creating puzzles and other active processes related to the literature to be learned. Students who were actively involved in creating the new material remembered the material significantly better than students who had passively read the material.

McNamara, D. S., Kintsch, E., Songer, N. B., & Kintsch, W. (1996). Are good texts always better? Interactions of text coherence, background knowledge, and levels of understanding in learning from text. *Cognition and Instruction, 14*(1), 1–43. doi:10.1207/s1532690xci1401_1

The investigators examined students' comprehension of one of four versions of a text. They found that readers who knew little about the topic of the text benefited from a strong, coherent text, whereas high-knowledge readers benefitted from a weak, minimally coherent text. The investigators argued that the poorly written text forced the knowledgeable readers to work harder to understand the unstated relationships in the text.

Workshop 1.1
Concept Maps

A map does not just chart, it unlocks and formulates meaning; it forms bridges between here and there, between disparate ideas that we did not know were previously connected.

—Reif Larsen,
The Selected Works of T. S. Spivet (2010)

Concept maps were initially created to improve learning in the sciences but are now also used as graphic organizers that illustrate relationships among ideas, images, or words. These maps function as visual displays of the hierarchal organization of ideas. They could also illustrate a process or a sequence of events similar to a flow chart. By establishing relationships and demonstrating how discrete ideas form a larger whole, the maps are a way to develop logical thinking and study skills.

Nilson (2010) notes that by asking students to fill in missing sections of an incomplete concept map, these maps can serve as assessment tools (see also Clark, 2011). If students are not familiar with creating a map, demonstrate the process to the class and then ask students to work in small groups to create a simple model. If a more colorful and less structured tool fits instructional needs, a mind map can work well. Mind maps and concept maps differ in that the first focuses on subtopics of one idea whereas the second connects relationships among multiple ideas. Both types of maps can be used to enhance motivation, attention, understanding, and recall through reflecting on connections between ideas.

Several good tutorials on creating concept maps are available on YouTube:

iMindMap. (2007, January 8). Maximise the power of your brain: Tony Buzan Mind Mapping [YouTube video]. Retrieved from http://www.youtube.com/watch?v=MlabrWv25qQ

Penn State University Libraries. (2013, January 17). How to create a concept map [YouTube video]. Retrieved from http://www.youtube.com/watch?v=eYtoZRmWLBc

University of Ontario Institute of Technology, Academic Success Centre. (2011, August 30). Concept maps—A visual study tool [YouTube video]. Retrieved from http://www .youtube.com/watch?v=vuBLI6ijHHg

University of Waterloo. (2011, May 3). Three concept map tools: CmapTools, VUE, and Mindmeister [YouTube video]. Retrieved from http://www.youtube.com/watch?v=PODBS-YbRcO&list=TLaeCperJK3vA

Western Washington University, Center for Instructional Innovation and Assessment. (2008, October 7). Classroom assessment technique: Concept maps [YouTube video]. Retrieved from http://www.youtube.com/watch?v=Gm1owfOuGFM

Uses of Concept Maps

Concept maps can be used in a variety of ways in the classroom:

1. To evaluate prior knowledge. Ask students to create a visual representation of what they know about an idea or concept.
2. To demonstrate how experts organize knowledge. Build a map that shows students how an expert learner thinks. (This exercise could also help in the course-design process.)
3. To summarize reading. Ask students to map ideas about an article, the main points of a chapter, or the theme of a novel in order to see relationships.

4. To plan a task. Have student groups visualize a project or lab assignment with a concept map in order to create an overview of the steps that are involved.
5. To assess learning. At the end of a unit or course, ask students to create a map to show what they have learned.

Instructional Applications

The following are some strategies for constructing concept maps (Clark, 2011; Nilson, 2010):

1. Identify the key concepts from the lecture or reading and put each one on a sticky note on a whiteboard. Place the main concept in the center. Then order concepts with the broadest ideas closest to the main topic. Circle concepts that have a relationship to each other. Draw dotted lines to indicate links or connections between concepts. (Maps can also be transferred to paper or software.)
2. Give students a partially constructed map to complete.
3. Create several maps over time, allowing students to see how their understanding changes.
4. Construct maps with reference to a "focus question" that specifies the problem or issue as a class.

Software programs such as CmapTools, MindManager, and Inspiration allow multiple users to work on a map at the same time.

Figure 1.1 A concept map on concept maps. Created by J. Novak on Cmaps, courtesy of the Institute for Human and Machine Cognition. Used with permission.

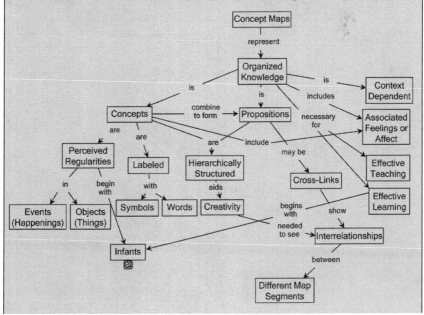

Annotated Research Studies

Daly, B. (2004). Using concept maps with adult students in higher education. In A. J. Cañas, J. D. Novak, & F. M. González (Eds.), *Concept maps: Theory, methodology, technology: Proceedings of the first international Conference on Concept Mapping* (Vol. 1, pp. 183–190). Retrieved from http://cmc.ihmc.us/cmc2004Proceedings/cmc2004%20-%20Vol%201.pdf

Two groups of graduate students were taught to use concept maps as a constructivist learning strategy. They were followed over the course of a year to see the impact concept mapping had on their learning. Results indicated that these students became significantly more aware of their own learning processes as well as their learning strategies than the control group.

Horton, P. B., McConney, A., Gallo, M., Woods, A., Senn, G., & Hamelin, D. (1993). An investigation of the effectiveness of concept mapping as an instructional tool. *Science Education, 77*(1), 95–111.

Nineteen studies were analyzed for the effect on test scores and student attitude. Test scores increased from the 50th percentile to the 68th percentile in classes using concept maps. Student attitudes toward classes when using concept maps were also significantly higher.

Zelik, M., Schau, C., Mattern, N., Hall, S., Teague, K., & Bisard, W. (1997). Conceptual astronomy: A novel model for teaching postsecondary science courses. *American Journal of Physics, 6*(10), 987–996. doi:10.1119/1.18702

In this experimental study, the astronomy students who developed concept maps scored higher than the control group on three kinds of conceptual examinations: the ability to relate concepts, a multiple-choice test of facts, and a fill-in-the-blank concept map.

Principle 2: Meaningful and Spaced Repetition Increases Retention

Repetitio mater memoriae.
[Repetition is the mother of memory.]
—Latin proverb

We are what we repeatedly do. Excellence, then, is not an act, but habit.
—Aristotle

Repetition is essential to learning because, as noted by Zull (2002), it is one way that short-term learning is converted into long-term memory (see

p. 3, this volume). When a memory is formed, a pathway is created between neurons. Just as a well-worn path becomes a road from continued use, the pathway between neurons is cultivated by reiterating and replicating ideas or skills (Reiser & Dempsey, 2007). By repeating deliberately, wisely, and (to avoid boredom) differently, educators increase the probability that learners will store information in their long-term memory, where it can be retrieved and applied when needed. Differences, or twists, in repetition could include reviewing new concepts by playing a game, working in pairs or small groups, or writing a 1-minute paper.

Learners acquire new information more effectively if it is introduced gradually and repeated in timed intervals (Kornell, 2009; Squire, 2004). This "distributed practice" benefits long-term retention more than learning material in close succession. Although students may achieve high scores on tests taken shortly after new material is presented, this is not an indicator of long-term retention. In fact, without sustained practice over time, new material is forgotten because it loses its meaning and there is no longer reason for it to be stored in long-term memory (Sousa, 2006). As current research has shown (Cepeda et al., 2006; Delaney, Verkoeijen, & Spirgel, 2010; Medina, 2008), spaced schedules of testing are key to long-term retention. Distributed practice "sustains meaning and consolidates the learning into long-term storage in a form that will ensure accurate recall and applications in the future" (Sousa, 2006, p. 99).

Instructional Applications

Encourage Distributed Practice Through Distributed Testing

Instructors can nudge students toward distributing their practice by distributing testing. Frequent testing can provide a strong incentive for regular review. Begin or end each class session with a review exercise. Student response instruments (clickers) can also be implemented for regular assessments (see Principle 6: Formative Assessment or Low-Stakes Evaluation Strengthens Retention, p. 43).

Break Down a Skill Into Parts Before Repeating and Practicing It

When a course involves learning a particular skill, such as giving an oral presentation, interviewing, or performing a piece on a musical instrument, divide the skill into its component parts. This allows students to know which parts of the skill need their attention, and they can then design ways to practice the skill through repetition. The famous golfer Tiger Woods practiced one skill, such as hitting golf balls out of sand traps, hundreds of times in one session to hone his technique (Medina, 2008).

Schedule Daily Study Sessions
Encourage students to schedule a 50-minute study session each day for every course. Once the semester gets rolling, adjustments may have to be made since courses demand different amounts of study time. By planning ahead, students will become accustomed to thinking in terms of distributed practice rather than cramming before an exam.

Use Student-Created Learning Tools
Encourage students to review by creating their own learning tools, such as flash cards, outlines, PowerPoint slides, or MP3s. These tools allow students to repeat, self-test, and review outside class material that they will need to recall on a quiz or exam. Interactive web-based sources are listed for these tools under Principle 6: Formative Assessment or Low-Stakes Evaluation Strengthens Retention (p. 43).

Annotated Research Studies

Bahrick, H. P. (1979). Maintenance of knowledge: Questions about memory we forgot to ask. *Journal of Experimental Psychology: General, 108*(3), 296–308.

In this classic study, students learned translations of Spanish words in one session and then participated in six additional sessions in which they retrieved and relearned (with feedback) the translations. Spaced practice was more effective than massed practice, and the longer the lag time the greater the benefit.

Cepeda, N. J., Pashler, H., Vul, E., Wixted, J. T., & Rohrer, D. (2006). Distributed practice in verbal recall tasks: A review and quantitative synthesis. *Psychological Bulletin, 132*, 354–380.

This meta-analysis of the distributed practice effect examined the findings of 317 experiments. Spaced learning events, as opposed to massed learning events, consistently showed benefits.

Dunlosky, J., Rawson, K., Marsh, E., Nathan, M., & Willingham, D. (2013). Improving students' learning with effective learning techniques: Promising directions from cognitive and educational psychology. *Psychological Science in the Public Interest, 14*(1), 4–58. doi:10.1177/1529100612453266

In this metastudy Dunlosky et al. summarize studies of distributed practice with multiple variables. The overall assessment is that spaced practice is effective and works in a wide variety of teaching and learning situations. Spaced practice is easy to implement and has been used successfully in a number of classroom studies. The optimal number of days between teaching sessions varies from student to student and from task to task, but the teaching strategy of distributed practice is strong.

Principle 3: Emotion and Relevance Deepen Learning

By actively solving relevant problems, exploring current case studies, and discussing local and newsworthy events through peer interaction, debate and dialogue, relevance can bring theory to life, and provide the motivation necessary to inspire deep and sustained learning in higher education.

—Natasha Kenny (2010)

Emotion is the on/off switch for learning. . . . The emotional brain, the limbic system, has the power to open or close access to learning, memory, and the ability to make connections.

—Priscilla Vail (2010)

The link between learning and emotion is powerful; emotion gets our attention. Our memories retain charged events for long periods. In a 2011 webinar, Nilson made this connection explicit when she asked participants to recall where they were a week ago Tuesday, a year ago on June 21, the evening of their previous birthday, and the day of the 9/11 tragedy. Of course, attendees were much more likely to remember their birthdays and the 9/11 tragedy. When we have learning experiences that involve emotion—whether it is fear, anger, excitement, drama, humor, or empathy—those experiences are more likely to be remembered. What is happening in the brain to trigger this memory? When the brain detects emotion, neurons release the chemical dopamine, which is like a "chemical Post-it note that says 'remember this'" (Medina, 2008, p. 81). That Post-it note ensures that the memory will be processed more deeply.

One way to make courses emotionally meaningful is to give students opportunities to connect course material to the world around them. For a 2008 article, Kember, Ho, and Hong interviewed students in nine undergraduate programs at three different universities in Hong Kong. The authors found that relevance of course material was the most prominent component for student motivation. Indeed, students were more eager to learn new material when professors established relevance by "showing how theory can be applied in practice, establishing relevance to local cases, relating material to everyday applications, or finding applications in current newsworthy issues" (p. 249).

Creating challenging assignments that allow students to be successful can have a powerful impact in the classroom. Positive and successful learning activities stimulate the brain to reward itself through the release of neurotransmitters such as dopamine and serotonin (Medina, 2008). When positive feelings are associated with new learning, additional synaptic connections are formed. These connections create additional circuits that help place new information into a framework of existing knowledge, which allows for greater recall (Medina, 2008; Rogan, Stäubli, & LeDoux, 1997; Zull, 2002).

We know from recent research (Braun & Bock, 2007; Caine, Caine, McClintic, & Klimek, 2005) that relevant learning experiences not only motivate students but also enhance student comprehension. When students can connect new information with a larger body of knowledge, they are better able to anchor the information into their long-term memory. Having multiple connections between what they are learning and what they already know also makes it easier for students to access new information when they need it (Nilson, 2010; Zull, 2002).

Instructional Applications

Create a Positive Environment

This may seem obvious, but work toward creating a positive environment in class. Take an interest in students, learn their names, and explain the purpose of the various teaching strategies to create relevance. A positive teacher attitude and passion for the topic go a long way in making learning pleasant and successful (see Workshop A.1: The Syllabus, p. 61).

Cultivate Emotion as an Instructor

Nilson (2010) invites educators to be "dramatic, humorous, surprising, maddening" and encourages them to allow students to reflect on and write down their responses to the material. "Any emotion will aid learning by inducing more enduring changes—that is, the generation of new, lasting synapses—in the brain" (p. 5).

Recognize Where Students Are Developmentally and Cognitively

As Ambrose, Bridges, DiPietro, Lovett, and Norman (2010) point out,

> As educators, we are primarily concerned with fostering intellectual and creative skills in our students, but we must recognize that students are not only intellectual, but also social and emotional beings, and that these dimensions interact within the classroom climate to influence learning and performance. (p. 156)

When we understand our students developmentally and cognitively, we can then find strategies to shape our classroom climate in appropriate ways.

Use Role Playing

A dry text can come to life when students are asked to take on the roles. This can easily work in a history class—students could become the characters they read about—but it also may work well in a science class. For example, in a biology class students could become atoms and interact with one another.

Increase Opportunities for Student Success
Give frequent low-stakes feedback to help foster an environment where it is safe to learn from one's errors.

Remember the Power of the Spoken Word
Students can read a poem but never really hear the poem. Read excerpts of powerful texts out loud and let students hear the emotion behind the words.

Lower Student Anxiety
Reminding learners of what they already know makes them feel less anxious and gives them a positive feeling about what they are learning.

Bait the Hook
"Bait the hook" throughout the class with concise narratives related to the topic. These examples could be humorous, moving, or provocative to (re)capture the students' attention.

Develop Review Games
Create a game that will review the concepts learned and simultaneously allow learners to feel successful. User-friendly templates for *Jeopardy!* and other games can be found in Overstreet (2007).

Tell a Story
Storytelling is often used as an attention grabber that can evoke positive emotions. There is good reason why telling an engaging story is a part of nearly every culture as a means of entertainment and education. Uses of storytelling include sharing history, personal narratives, political commentary, and evolving cultural norms.

Make It Relevant
Share a photo or a newspaper or magazine clipping that connects the topic to current events, pop culture, or student interests in order to increase student motivation. Create learning activities based on topics that are highly engaging and relevant to your students' lives and that activate prior knowledge. Ask them to provide relevant examples from their experiences.

Annotated Research Studies

Ainley, M. (2006). Connecting with learning: Motivation, affect and cognition in interest processes. *Educational Psychological Review, 18,* 391–405.

Using interactive software, the researcher monitored dynamic states and behaviors while subjects learned tasks. This study demonstrates the possible relationship between student interest and alertness, attention, and concentration.

Dolan, R. J. (2002). Emotion, cognition, and behavior. *Science, 298*(5596), 1191–1194. doi:10.1126/science.1076358

This article explores the neurobiological substrates of emotion and interrogates the ways in which emotion interacts with cognition. It describes the broad outline of the brain structures that regulate emotion. Educators may find the sections on "Emotions Perception and Attention" and "Emotion, Memory and Learning" useful.

Kember, D., Ho, A., & Hong, C. (2008). The importance of establishing relevance in motivating student learning. *Active Learning in Higher Education, 9*(3), 249–263.

In this study 36 students were interviewed about motivation, and the authors found that students had less motivation if a course was based on theory alone. When students understood how the theory could be applied to the discipline or profession, they became more motivated. Guest speakers, field trips, CBL, and problem-based learning can all establish relevance and motivate student learning.

Pekrun, R., Goetz, T., Titz, W., & Perry, R. (2002). Academic emotions in students' self-regulated learning and achievement: A program of qualitative and quantitative research. *Educational Psychologist, 37*(2), 91–106.

This study demonstrates that there is a rich diversity of academic emotions. To date, most research has centered on text anxiety. The authors use a self-report instrument called the Academic Emotions Questionnaire to measure students' emotions of enjoyment, hope, pride, relief, anger, anxiety, shame, hopelessness, and boredom. The results indicate a significant relationship between students' academic emotions and their "motivation, learning strategies, cognitive resources, self-regulation, and academic achievement" (p. 91).

Shultz, P., & Pekrun, R. (Eds.). (2007). *Emotion in education.* Burlington, MA: Academic Press.

Scholars from around the world contributed chapters on aspects of emotion and learning for this book. The authors describe the current state of research on emotion and learning and posit questions for future study. The book is divided into three sections: the first integrates current theory, questions, and methodologies regarding emotion and learning; the second focuses on students' emotions; and the third focuses on the importance of professors' emotions in an academic context. Contributors have different perspectives, but in most chapters the authors have described specific emotions and their potential outcomes. The final chapter explores future directions for the field.

Workshop 3.1
Community-Based Learning

Community-based learning is experiential education in which students engage in activities that address human and community needs together with structured opportunities intentionally designed to promote student learning and development. Reflection and reciprocity are key concepts of [community-based] learning.

—Barbara Jacoby (1996)

CBL, also known as service-learning, is a powerful strategy to make the classroom come alive. It is important to remember that CBL differs from both volunteerism (which focuses on community benefit) and internships (which focus on student benefits). Ideally, CBL should be equally beneficial to the student and the community. CBL works best in the context of a rigorous academic experience. Instructors are encouraged to include a strong academic component that incorporates guiding and challenging the students to process the material and relate it to course content.

Instructors often regard community experiences in the same way they do a traditional text. CBL can function as a primary, supplementary, or optional text. In a traditional course, students are not normally graded on having completed the reading; instead, they are graded on how they demonstrate the knowledge via tests, papers, and presentations. CBL can work in a similar way—students are graded not for time they spend in the community, but rather for the quality of their academic experience.

Implementing Community-Based Learning

Instructors who are planning to implement CBL are encouraged to consider the following (Howard, 2013–2014):

- *Learning objectives.* Whether creating a new course or revising one, CBL needs to match learning objectives.
- *Role in the course.* Decide what role CBL will play in the course. Will CBL act as a supplemental activity in your course, or will it play a central role? Best practices indicate that CBL is most rewarding when it is a significant component in the course.
- *Community.* Speak with leaders in the community that will be served. Make sure the project will benefit the community in a meaningful way.
- *Time frame.* Allow ample time for planning and executing the project. Generally, it is best to have planned the project and contacted the partnering organization before the semester starts.

- *Student needs.* Students need training and orientation before they begin their project. Also, students need to understand why they are participating in CBL.
- *Paperwork.* Before students start their projects, they may need to have background checks or other paperwork done. Make sure they are informed about what paperwork they will need and can begin the process early in the semester.
- *Plan for assessment.* Have a clear plan for how students will be assessed in the academic component of the CBL project.

Instructional Applications

Sociology

In a sociology class at Colby College, teams of students met with community leaders, executives, development directors, and boards of nonprofits to get an insider's view of nonprofits. These student teams then took on the challenge of writing fundable grants for their partnering agency. The entire class also acted as a foundation, with a mission statement and parameters for giving grants. Finally, the class reviewed the grant applications and voted on a fundable grant. Through the Learn by Giving and the Sunshine Lady Foundation, the class had $10,000 of real money to be divided among the best proposals. Students were able not only to identify needs in the community and partner with nonprofits but also to understand how funding for worthy causes is given or denied. For more information see Meader (2011).

Environmental Studies

As a capstone experience, students partner with a local agency involved with environmental issues to determine a question of interest. They then collect and analyze data and present their findings to the community. The community members themselves ultimately decide how they want to proceed.

Spanish

In a Spanish conversation class, students work with children in a local Hispanic community—in an afterschool program, as tutors, or as mentors. For their culminating activity, they reflect on their service and what they learned by producing videos about the experience. They then watch their peers' videos and have a class discussion as a final reflection.

Annotated Resources

Boyer, E. (1996). The scholarship of engagement. *Bulletin of the American Academy of Arts and Sciences, 1*(1), 18–33.

Boyer makes a powerful argument for engaged learning, stating that "scholarship has to prove its worth not on its own terms, but in its service to the nation and the world." Excerpts from this article may help students understand why they are being assigned a service project and its importance in the classroom.

Bringle, R., Philips, M., & Hudson, M. (2004). *The measure of service learning: Research scales to assess student experiences.* Washington, DC: American Psychological Association.

This book provides scales to measure the impact of service-learning. It offers scales to measure such things as critical thinking, moral development, and attitudes.

Campus Compact. (2003). *Introduction to service learning toolkit: Readings and resources for faculty.* Boston, MA: Author.

This is an invaluable book for those interested in service-learning. It offers information on learning theory and the pedagogy of CBL, as well as practical guidance for those interested in implementing service-learning in their classes.

Correia, M., & Bleicher, R. (2008). Making connections to teach reflection. *Michigan Journal of Community Service Learning, 14*(12), 41–49.

The authors discuss ways in which effective reflection can be taught and offer detailed guidelines for teachers to help their students get the most out of the process.

Felten, P., Gilchrist, L. Z., & Darby, A. (2006). Emotion and learning: Feeling our way toward a new theory of reflection in service-learning. *Michigan Journal of Community Service Learning, 12*(2), 38–46.

This article stresses the importance of recognizing how dialogue between the emotional and the intellectual form the experience and methodology of service-learning.

Hatcher, J. A., Bringle, R. G., & Muthiah, R. (2004). Designing effective reflection: What matters to service-learning? *Michigan Journal of Community Service Learning, 11*(1), 38–46.

This study reports on a multicampus research survey that asked students how emotion and reflection were implemented in their service-learning courses. The results indicated that integrating an academic component with a structured reflective component significantly improved the quality of the course.

Howard, K. (2013–2014). *Community based learning at Centre College: Faculty handbook.* Retrieved from Centre College Center for Teaching and Learning website: http://ctl .centre.edu/assets/cblhandbook.pdf

This handbook is an excellent resource for professors and students who want to engage in service-learning. It also offers examples of CBL across the disciplines and has links to sample syllabi. Although the handbook offers sound pedagogical reasons to implement service-learning, it also offers practical tips—including forms students need to complete and sample contracts with partner organizations.

Jacoby, B. (Ed.). (1996). *Service-learning in higher education.* San Francisco, CA: Jossey-Bass.

This book of fourteen essays analyzes the theoretical approaches to service-learning and provides practical means of implementation.

Videos

The following are brief videos illustrating examples of CBL:

Mount Holyoke College. (2010, March 17). Community-based learning at MHC [YouTube video]. Retrieved from http://www.youtube.com/watch?v=wB5_5X4w_-8

University of Notre Dame, Center for Social Concerns. (2012, October 30). ROLL and CSC community-based learning [YouTube video]. Retrieved from http://www.youtube.com/watch?v=i4YbxoOICwA

Online Resources

Generator School Network's National Service-Learning Clearinghouse, http://gsn.nylc.org/clearinghouse

This database offers syllabi, lesson plans, and project ideas for those who want to include CBL as a component of their course.

Learning by Giving Foundation, www.learningbygivingfoundation.org

This foundation promotes "the teaching of effective charitable giving." It supports rigorous, full-credit courses with grants of $10,000 that can be distributed to local nonprofits.

Michigan Journal of Community Service Learning, http://ginsberg.umich.edu/mjcsl/

This link gives access to past and present articles from the *Michigan Journal of Community Service Learning*. The journal is peer-reviewed and focuses on the research, theory, pedagogy, and practice of service-learning.

2

ACTIVELY ENGAGED
LEARNING

Learning is not a spectator sport. Students do not learn by sitting in class listening to teachers, memorizing prepackaged assignments, or spitting out answers. They must talk about what they are learning, write about it, relate it to past experiences, and apply it to their daily lives. They must make what they learn a part of themselves.

—Joseph R. Codde (2006)

The one who does the work is the one who does the learning.

—Terry Doyle (2008)

Chapter 2 synthesizes research about active learning and offers ways to engage students both inside and outside class time. We pay special attention to multisensory teaching and group learning. Workshops in this section present strategies to flip the classroom, asking students to view mini-lectures before class, and provide guidelines for using both problem-based learning (PBL) and process-oriented guided-inquiry learning (POGIL).

Engaged Learning

People learn most effectively when they are engaged in a meaningful and challenging activity. As Nilson (2010) points out, "The human brain can't focus for long when it is in a passive state" (p. 4). Students need to work to solve problems so that they can both teach themselves and construct a new understanding of the material. By being challenged and actively grappling with the subject, students learn more deeply (see Principle 1: Desirable Difficulties Increase Long-Term Retention, p. 5). Recent research indicates that the benefits of using interactive engagement strategies are considerable. Hake (1998) found that test scores evaluating conceptual understanding were almost twice as high for students in classes that used engaged learning methods than for those in traditional classes. Prince (2004) concluded that the "magnitude of improvements resulting from active-engagement methods" (p. 28) is significant. In addition, Brewer and Burgess (2005) found that students are more motivated to attend classes when active-learning strategies are used as opposed to classes that are solely lecture based.

In the last few decades, educators have become aware of many active-learning strategies (e.g., role playing, group work). It is important to remember, however, that *active learning* can be defined as "any instructional method that engages students in the learning process" (Prince, 2004, p. 28). That means that tried and true methods such as asking questions, taking notes, drawing, writing, and testing are actively engaging students. Indeed, using several of these methods to teach the same material activates different areas of the brain, giving students the opportunity to learn more deeply (Nilson, 2010).

One of the keys to engaged learning is to help students realize they are not solely looking for an answer but instead are discovering a process. Discovery occurs when learners act and take control of their own learning. Initially, this process may feel uncomfortable to some students. To address possible student resistance, instructors are encouraged to make their goals for using active-learning strategies explicit. When students understand that instructors value both process and product, they may be more comfortable exploring and executing new ideas.

Annotated Research Studies

Hake, R. (1998). Interactive-engagement vs. traditional methods: A six-thousand-student survey of mechanics test data for introductory physics courses. *American Journal of Physics, 66*(1), 64–74. doi:10.1119/1.18809

Pre- and posttest data for more than 6,000 students in introductory physics courses were analyzed. Students in classes where engaged learning techniques were used scored twice as high on tests measuring concepts than those in traditional classes.

Pascarella, E. T., & Terenzini, P. T. (2005). *How college affects students: Vol. 2. A third decade of research.* San Francisco, CA: Jossey-Bass.

Conducting a meta-analysis of hundreds of empirical studies, authors found that active-learning approaches provided a significant advantage over passive-learning approaches in terms of acquiring subject matter knowledge and academic skills.

Prince, M. (2004). Does active learning work? A review of the research. *Journal of Engineering Education, 93*(3), 223–231.

In this review of literature on active learning, the author found that students remember more content if lectures include brief activities rather than focus on covering the most material. He found that although the results vary in strength, there is broad support for active, collaborative, cooperative, and problem-based learning.

Wood, W. B., & Gentile, J. M. (2003). Teaching in a research context. *Science, 302*(5650), 1510. doi:10.1126/science.1091803

Physics, chemistry, and biology educators developed and used objective tests to compare student learning gains in traditional courses and in courses that used active engagement methods. The results provided substantial evidence that students acquired and integrated new knowledge more effectively in courses that included active, inquiry-based, and cooperative learning and courses that incorporated information technology, rather than in traditional courses.

Principle 4: Multisensory Instruction Deepens Learning

Our senses evolved to work together—vision influencing hearing, for example—which means that we learn best if we stimulate several senses at once.
—John Medina (2008)

A picture is worth a thousand words.
—Unknown

Investigators in large metastudies have concluded that multisensory teaching and learning can be more effective than traditional, unimodal teaching and learning (Fadel, 2008; Kress, Jewitt, Ogborn, & Charalampos, 2006; Medina, 2008; Tindall-Ford, Chandler, & Sweller, 1997). According to Nilson (2010), "Students learn new material best when they encounter it multiple times and through multiple teaching and learning strategies and multiple input modes" (p. 4). Learners cannot focus for long in a passive state (Jones-Wilson, 2005; Svinicki, 2004). Multisensory teaching activates different parts of the brain, which allows the brain to encode a memory more deeply. The more elaborately a memory is developed, the more meaningful the learning will be because the learner has to work harder to process information.

Teaching using multiple senses is different from teaching to "learning preferences" or "learning styles." Teaching to learning styles matches instruction to the students' supposed learning style (e.g., visual, auditory, read/write, or kinesthetic). In recent years a number of studies have shown this practice to be ineffective (Delahoussaye, 2002; Pashler, McDaniel, Rohrer, & Bjork, 2008).

Approaching a concept from multiple angles and asking students to use more than one of their senses strengthen their overall understanding. Our senses evolved to work together, so we learn best if we involve several senses. For example, adding visuals to text or auditory input can lead to considerable improvements in learning (Fadel, 2008; Medina, 2008). Several studies have demonstrated that after three days participants remembered only 10% of information received via auditory input. However, when a picture was added to this input, participants remembered 65% of the information (Kalyuga, 2000; Mayer & Gallini, 1990).

Functional magnetic resonance imaging (fMRI) scans demonstrate that our brains process visual, textual, and auditory input in separate channels, allowing for "simultaneous reinforcement of learning" (Fadel, 2008, p. 13). Teaching using the visual sense leads to deeper, more conceptual learning because visuals can provide cues to better understand how concepts are related. Visuals help learners both retain information for longer periods and retrieve it more easily (Medina, 2008; Pieters & Wedel, 2004; Stenberg, 2006; Vekiri, 2002).

When engaging students in complex multisensory tasks, instructors are encouraged to give students time to reflect and process in order to avoid cognitive overload (Kalyuga, 2000). In-class writing exercises or group work or simply turning to write on the board gives students a moment to review and assimilate new learning. Moreover, the senses do not need to be simultaneously stimulated; they can be sequentially stimulated. For example, an instructor may decide to begin with a lecture and then follow with discussion or an activity. In this way, students use more than one of their senses to reinforce their learning.

Instructional Applications

Create Opportunities to Hear, Read, Write About, See, Talk About, Act Out, Think About, and Touch New Material
Involve as many senses as possible when planning teaching for enhanced student learning. Encourage students to create concept maps or mind maps

(see Workshop 1.1: Concept Maps, p. 9), work in pairs or groups, free-write, take a practice quiz, or solve a problem (Nilson, 2010). Introduce a concept with one modality and then reinforce student learning by using a different modality. For example, begin class with a discussion and then reinforce student learning by adding a visual or a kinesthetic element.

Use PowerPoint Effectively

Keep in mind when creating a PowerPoint presentation that a picture really is worth 1,000 words. Instructors are encouraged to use more images and less text to make these presentations memorable and to increase retention (Mayer & Gallini, 1990; Medina, 2008; Pieters & Wedel, 2004; Stenberg, 2006; Vekiri, 2002).

Create a Barometer or Human Graph

After students have read a text or have heard a short lecture, ask them to move their desks out of the way (this exercise will require use of the whole room). Designate one end of the room as the "agree" area and the opposite end as the "disagree" area. Tell students that they will hear a series of statements and will need to decide whether they agree with them or not. To indicate that they agree with a statement, the students should stand in the "agree" area; if they disagree, they should stand in the "disagree" area. The students may also stand anywhere between the two extremes. Students must defend their position, but they can also move if they are convinced by their peers' arguments. Have students respond in this way to several statements before they return to their seats for a more in-depth discussion. This exercise requires not only that students have read the text before class but also that they listen to their peers' opinions during discussion.

Create Posters

By creating paper or virtual posters, students are encouraged to both synthesize material and use more than one of their senses. Have students examine a number of posters and then select criteria for making their own. Next, either as individuals or in small groups, they can design their posters. Once students have a basic design, allow them time to get peer feedback on their work via a gallery walk around the room. Students can then present their posters either for the class or for other students in their discipline (National Council of Teachers of English, 2004).

Reenact Material

Encourage students to bring costumes and props to class to reenact scenes from historical or literary texts or ethnographies. For example, students can wear costumes, introduce themselves as a historical figure, and take questions about their contributions to a particular historical movement. Or, as an alternative, students can hold a debate, but they must base their arguments on their character's beliefs or writings. This requires that students have a firm grasp of the writings or actions of their character before arriving in class.

Use PechaKucha

PechaKucha, pronounced "pe/chahk/cha," is Japanese for "chit chat." The concept was developed in Tokyo in 2003 by two architects as a new way to deliver PowerPoint presentations. In PechaKucha 20 slides, each shown for 20 seconds—for a total of 6 minutes 40 seconds—are advanced automatically as the speaker presents. This practice follows the brain-friendly guideline of grouping or chunking information into short learning segments. It also requires that the presenter work to distill content to the most important points. PechaKucha is most effective when one uses more graphics and very few words on each slide. Short discussion periods should follow each presentation. Encourage students to talk with one another about the information, not just ask the presenter questions. The discussion period helps students to process the new information and connect it to prior knowledge. For more information see Jung (n.d.). To watch successful PechaKucha presentations, see www.pechakucha.org/watch.

Ask Students to Give Micro-TED Talks

Invite students to give short TED talks on assigned topics. A suggested length of time is 4 minutes. Setting a time limit requires students to prioritize their points. Encourage students to illustrate their talk with a poster that can be displayed in the room and shared via a gallery walk to review the topics. Instructors may wish to have students record a practice session of their talks and evaluate their performance before their talk is to be given. In this way students are required to practice, and they can also determine what still needs rehearsal before they give their talk to the class. (Also see strategies included in Principle 3: Emotion and Relevance Deepen Learning, p. 15; Principle 5: Small Groups Engage Students, p. 32; and Principle 6: Formative Assessment or Low-Stakes Evaluation Strengthens Retention, p. 43.)

Annotated Research Studies

Ginns, P. (2005). Meta-analysis of the modality effect. *Learning and Instruction, 15,* 313–331.

Ginns reviewed 43 experimental studies and found that students who learned from instructional materials that combined graphics and spoken texts performed significantly better than students who learned from graphics with printed text.

Mayer, R. E. (2005). Cognitive theory of multimedia learning. In R. E. Mayer (Ed.), *Cambridge handbook of multimedia learning* (pp. 31–48). New York, NY: Cambridge University Press.

Mayer presents rules for more effective use of multimedia presentations. He also advocates using both pictures and text close together on the screen, but without extraneous information.

Pashler, H., McDaniel, M., Rohrer, D., & Bjork, R. (2008). Learning styles: Concepts and evidence. *Psychological Science in the Public Interest, 9*(3), 105–119. doi:10.1111/j.1539-6053.2009.01038.x

This metareport did not find sufficient evidence to justify matching teaching to specific learning style assessments.

Tindall-Ford, S., Chandler, P., & Sweller, J. (1997). When two sensory modes are better than one. *Journal of Experimental Psychology: Applied, 3*(4), 257–287. doi:10.1037/1076-898X.3.4.257

The results of this study indicate that when participants incorporated audio text and visual diagrams into their study, they performed better than those who studied using only visual tools.

Workshop 4.1
The Flipped Classroom

The flipped classroom is a pedagogical model in which the typical lecture and homework elements of a course are reversed. Short video lectures are viewed by students at home before the class session, while in-class time is devoted to exercises, projects, or discussions.

—EDUCAUSE (2013)

In a flipped class, students watch a brief, 10-minute screencast or short narrated video—usually created by their instructor—posted on a college course management website, such as Moodle or Blackboard. During class time, rather than listening to a content-heavy lecture, students work as a class or in small groups analyzing and applying key concepts. Their preparation outside class gives more time to interact with their peers and their instructor during class. In other words, the flipped classroom promotes hands-on, inquiry-based learning and gets students actively engaged in content-rich courses. Students both contribute to and assess their own learning in a meaningful way. This pedagogical model can be used either occasionally or on a regular basis throughout the semester, depending on the needs of the instructor and the class. An additional advantage of the flipped classroom is it allows the opportunity to have students approach a concept from multiple angles, which promotes deeper learning (see Principle 4: Multisensory Instruction Deepens Learning, p. 25).

Experienced "flippers" say that the assessment step is key to the success of this strategy. Asking students to take a short quiz either before class (electronically) or at the beginning of class allows instructors to quickly gather information about student understanding and tailor activities to meet students' learning needs (see Principle 6: Formative Assessment or Low-Stakes Evaluation Strengthens Retention, p. 43). The instructor then has the choice of giving a mini-lecture in class focusing on the most difficult parts of the material, making connections, or helping students conceptualize the material when they need guidance.

Some instructors assign homework related to the video due at the beginning of class. If students get a question wrong, they must rewatch that segment of the video. In fact, one advantage to a flipped class is students can view the professor's lecture as many times as needed in order to grasp complex concepts. Students can also engage in active-learning activities that require them to apply new information. For example, they could be asked to participate in a "Numbered Heads Together" activity (see p. 35) and then journal about how they reached their answers.

Although the flipped or reversed classroom has received a lot of attention in the past few years as an exciting new teaching and learning strategy, the basic premise of preparing before class is not new. What is new is that the technology that students are already using enables instructors to create short narrated videos for students to observe and study prior to attending class. (Some examples of this technology and software are provided at the end of this chapter.)

Annotated Research Studies

Bodie, G., Powers, W., & Fitch-Hauser, M. (2006, August). Chunking, priming and active learning: Toward an innovative and blended approach to teaching communication-related skills. *Interactive Learning Environments, 14*(2), 119–135.

The research on priming and memory indicates that when students have received direct instruction before class, they are "primed" for active-learning activities that will take place in a flipped classroom and will then have better recall of facts. The prior experience with the stimuli increases learning.

Finkel, E. (2012). Flipping the script in K12. Retrieved from District Administration website: http://www.districtadministration.com/article/flipping-script-k12

In this study the failure rate of students in a high school mathematics class in Michigan dropped from 44% to 13% after adopting flipped classrooms.

Flipped Learning Network. (2012). Improve student learning and teacher satisfaction with one flip of the classroom. Retrieved from http://flippedlearning1.files.wordpress.com/2012/07/classroomwindowinfographic7-12.pdf

This article indicates that currently there is not strong scientific data indicating the effectiveness of the flipped classroom. However, 453 instructors who had flipped their classes were surveyed, and 67% found that their students' test scores were higher and 80% reported improved student attitudes. Ninety percent of the instructors said they would flip their classrooms again.

Videos

Crowder College. (2013, April 24). The flipped classroom—Crowder College [YouTube video]. Retrieved from http://www.youtube.com/watch?v=r8mMi0-u2lw

Durley, C., Janke, P., & Johnson, G. (2012, May 14). The flipped classroom as a vehicle to the future [YouTube video]. Retrieved from http://www.youtube.com/watch?v=ZpHfTO8SW7U

Wilmot, J. (2013, January 16). How to flip the classroom [YouTube video]. Retrieved from http://www.youtube.com/watch?v=IjUtSvGvB-0&feature=endscreen

Online Resources

Aune, S. P. (2008, February 21). 12 screencasting tools for creating video tutorials. Retrieved from Mashable: http://mashable.com/2008/02/21/screencasting-video-tutorials/

EDUCAUSE. (2013). 7 things you should know about flipped classrooms. Retrieved from http://www.educause.edu/library/resources/7-things-you-should-know-about-flipped-classrooms

Software

Jing from Techsmith (limited to 5 minutes), http://www.techsmith.com/jing.html
Panopto, http://panopto.com
Screenr, http://www.screenr.com/
Screencast-o-matic, http://www.screencast-o-matic.com/

Principle 5: Small Groups Engage Students

*In the long history of humankind (and animal kind, too)
those who learned to collaborate and improvise
most effectively have prevailed.*

—Charles Darwin

*Individual commitment to a group effort—that is
what makes a team work, a company work,
a society work, a civilization work.*

—Vince Lombardi, head coach of the 1959–1967
Green Bay Packers

Hundreds of studies have found that students who were engaged in group work displayed deeper learning, higher academic achievement with difficult assignments, and increased student responsibility than students who worked alone (Johnson, Johnson, & Smith, 1991, p. 98; Millis, 2010; Nilson, 2010, p. 156; Prince, 2004; Wenzel, 2000). These studies used different methodologies and included participants from different socioeconomic classes, ethnicities, and cultural backgrounds. Although the results varied in statistical strength, the studies indicated that when compared with students exposed to traditional means of instruction, students who learned in small groups "exhibited better reasoning and critical thinking skills, proposed more new ideas and solutions when presented with problems, and transferred more of what they learned in prior situations to new problems" (Wenzel, 2000, p. 295A). Moreover, engaged learning in group work has been found to be successful in motivating female and minority students to become involved in math and science (Johnson et al., 1991; Wenzel, 2000).

Group work is also called collaborative learning, cooperative learning, and peer instruction. Since the late 1990s, medical schools and the sciences have been using carefully designed team-learning methods, such as PBL and POGIL. These structured methods are devised to teach both content and writing skills through collaboration, using an inquiry-based learning approach (Farrell, Moog, & Spencer, 1999). We have devoted Workshops 5.1 and 5.2 to exploring these topics because of their complexity.

Strategies for working in small groups do not have to be highly structured to be effective. Students can play a variety of roles in group work from having specific responsibilities in more complex group assignments to simply partnering in a think-pair-share exercise. Think-pair-share (see p. 34, this volume) is easy to implement and can quickly change the energy in the room by getting everyone talking; moreover, it primes the pump for a productive discussion. To break up a lecture, instructors can divide students into groups to solve a challenging problem.

Group work can serve as a major semester assignment, a lecture break, or an assessment tool. However instructors decide to use group work, it is helpful to the students if they understand the goal. When students understand the reason behind working in groups and the instructor's expectations, they are less likely to resist these activities. (See the annotated resources for Principle 5, p. 37, for strategies for assessing group work.) In this way instructors remind students of course content, establish expectations for active learning, and help students understand why professors aren't lecturing for the entire class period. With thoughtful implementation, cooperative learning can be a powerful tool in the professor's toolbox.

Instructor-Created Groups

Heller and Hollabaugh (1992) found that instructor-created groups that were heterogeneous in ability and gender promoted better learning and development of social skills. Long-term groups, in particular, performed better with fewer issues of cronyism when instructors created the groups. Weimer (2010) suggests that instructors take into account student skills, previous experiences, and background knowledge when creating groups. One means of gathering this information is through a prior knowledge survey.

Conversely, Chapman, Meuter, Toy, and Wright (2006) found that self-selection of groups in an accounting class fostered better group dynamics, more positive attitudes toward the group experience, and better group outcomes. Hilton and Phillips (2010) found that "although student-selected groups perceived they produced higher-quality work, the actual grades assigned to the group projects did not differ between group formation conditions" (p. 26). In summary, instructors are encouraged to invite students to form their own groups for short-term assignments intended to energize the class but to create instructor-created groups for longer-term projects.

For more information about forming groups, see Weimer (2011).

Instructional Applications

Fishbowl

With this exercise students respond to a controversial claim made by the instructor, but only students sitting inside the "fishbowl" may talk. Students outside the fishbowl listen to arguments and prepare to enter. To set up the exercise, place several chairs (two to six, depending on the size of the class) in a circle in the middle of a classroom with one to three empty chairs just outside the circle. The rest of the class sits in a larger circle around the fishbowl.

When students outside the fishbowl want to talk, they must go to one of the empty ("on-deck") chairs just outside the circle. Several variations on this exercise are possible: (a) all students can be required to take a turn in the fishbowl by the end of the exercise; (b) students can be asked to prepare for the activity by writing a response to the initial claim before the fishbowl begins; and (c) students observing the fishbowl can be required to take notes for a post-fishbowl discussion.

Jigsaw
In a jigsaw exercise, students are divided into groups of four to six. During the first phase of the activity, each group reads or researches a different topic in order to become experts on that topic. During the second phase, the experts on a single topic are separated. New groups comprising students who have researched other areas of interest are formed, and students coach one another on their assigned topics. For example, in a literature class, the instructor might divide the class into five groups. One group might be assigned symbolism in the reading while another group works on imagery. Each group refines and researches one concept, and every group member is expected to become an "expert." It is helpful to have the groups devise ways of presenting their content area to others. In the second phase, each of the new groups now has an "expert" on one of the assigned topics. All students in each group are then responsible for teaching their concept.

Think-Pair-Share
The instructor poses a question requiring reflection and gives students time to think through and possibly write an appropriate response. Each student then turns to a partner and shares his or her reflections. Finally, students share their responses (and possibly the responses of their partners) with the class. A variation on this strategy is "think-pair-scare," in which students take a short quiz after reviewing with a partner.

Deck of Cards
Students enter the classroom and take a card from the deck. All students who have the same number will be in a group together that day. When group work is first used in a class, students are often relieved to be assigned to a group rather than having to find their own partners. Also, randomly assigning groups eliminates the tendency for students to work with the same people.

Case Studies or Case-Based Learning
Cases introduce students to challenging, real-world situations. Students are asked to apply what they have learned in class in order to analyze the case and to devise workable solutions. The cases should be well structured but lack an

obvious or clear solution. Case-based learning is similar to PBL (see Workshop 5.1, p. 38), but PBL problems tend to be "messier and fuzzier" (Nilson, 2010, p. 187) and course material alone cannot provide viable solutions.

Numbered Heads Together

Divide students into groups of four and assign each student a number. Ask a question or pose a problem and allow the students time for discussion. Call out a number. The students with that number summarize what their group has discussed. This exercise demands that everyone in the group participate and be ready to speak (Nilson, 2010).

Send a Problem

For this exercise instructors divide the class into groups containing four or five students. Each group receives an envelope with a different problem attached. The groups discuss their problem, and at the end of the allotted time, they put their solutions into the envelope and give it to another group. The next group tries to solve the problem without looking at the solution in the envelope. After time is called, the groups again pass their problems to another group. The last group opens the envelope and then analyzes, evaluates, and synthesizes the proposed solutions in order to present their peers with best approaches and answers.

Document Sharing

Use document sharing in a program such as Google Docs to have students edit one another's writing. Document sharing also allows the instructor to track student work.

Heterogeneous Skill Groups

Mix up the skill levels in groups so that students can teach and learn from one another. For example, in a calculus class a professor assigns groups based on the amount of math students have taken prior to the class. Four or five weeks into the semester, she makes new heterogeneous groups based on students' performance in the class, and five weeks later she changes the groups again. This helps students learn to work with many of their classmates and also allows groups to change, avoiding difficult group dynamics.

Round

Form groups of four to six students. Each student has a limited amount of time—for example, 2 or 3 minutes—to express his or her point of view on a given topic. A group scribe records responses and then reports these to the class. This strategy is used to elicit a range of viewpoints and to build a sense of safe participation (Angelo & Cross, 1993).

Peer Writing in Groups

Students read and respond to one another's drafts for a writing assignment. For these groups to be productive, the instructor needs to help students set up specific procedures and objectives. For example, students need to know what they must prepare, how the groups will be organized, and what their group's goal will be. For a good resource on peer writing group guidelines, see George Mason University (n.d.).

Inkshedding

This is a technique for peer review in which students write a response to a question, news event, or class discussion. They then pass their text to another student who highlights the most striking or intriguing passages. The most often marked passages are then transcribed and distributed in the next class for discussion. See Sargent (n.d.).

Speed Dating

Form two concentric circles with chairs in the outer circle facing the chairs in the inner circle in pairs. Once they are seated, students are given a topic to discuss, and the instructor sets a timer, usually for 2–8 minutes. When the timer sounds, those seated in the outer circle move clockwise. This continues until every person in the outer circle has spoken with every person in the inner circle. This activity is especially useful at the beginning of class, as it allows students to generate ideas with their peers before discussing them in a more complex way with the entire class.

Team-Based Learning

Team-based learning (TBL) is a strategy that uses long-term and instructor-assigned groups of five to seven students with diverse skill sets and backgrounds. Students complete assigned reading and homework before taking a quiz in class (a "readiness assurance process"). Immediately afterward, students take the same quiz again with members of their group, this time working on a single answer sheet. Students can appeal answers that their team missed citing statements in the reading to support their arguments. While most of the class is devoted to small-group activities, the instructor can also build on questions raised during class discussion. Teams are awarded points for working well together. Points are withheld when a team member does not contribute. Learning how to work, interact, and collaborate in a team is essential for success in this kind of environment. The instructor's role changes from being the "expert" to facilitating the learning process. For more information on TBL, see Plank (2011) and www .teambasedlearning.org.

Annotated Resources

Johnson, D. W., Johnson, R. T., & Smith, K. A. (1998). Cooperative learning returns to college: What evidence is there that it works? *Change, 20*(4), 26–35.

The investigators examined 168 studies of cooperative learning conducted over 73 years. They found that group learning is almost 150% as effective as individual or competitive learning in acquisition and retention of knowledge, problem-solving skills, higher-level reasoning, and verbal tasks. Moreover, when engaged in cooperative learning, students demonstrate persistence, a willingness to take on difficult tasks, and higher motivation. They are also better able to transfer learning from one situation to another.

Lord, T. R. (2001). 101 reasons for using cooperative learning in biology teaching. *American Biology Teacher, 6*(1), 30–38.

This article elucidates the reasons for incorporating peer learning in classes and backs up assertions with citations from research on group learning. For example, the author cites a study published in Richard Light's 1990 Harvard Assessment Seminars report in which it was shown that students in teams did significantly better in all measures of their biology course than students who studied alone. Light also reported that students in teams spoke more often, asked more questions, and were more engaged in biology than those in nongrouped, teacher-directed classes.

Slavin, R. (1991). Synthesis of research on cooperative learning. *Educational Leadership, 48*(5), 71–82. Retrieved from http://www.ascd.org/ASCD/pdf/journals/ed_lead/el_199102_slavin.pdf

Seventy studies that compared classes taught using cooperative learning with classes using traditional methods for more than 4 weeks were reviewed. Forty-one of the studies, or 61%, found that students in classes using cooperative-learning approaches significantly outperformed students in traditional classes. This study also found that the most successful cooperative-learning teaching strategies involved group goals and individual accountability.

Williamson, V. M., & Rowe, M. W. (2002). Group problem-solving versus lecture in college-level quantitative analysis: The good, the bad, and the ugly. *Journal of Chemical Education, 79*(9), 1131–1134.

In this study one section of a chemistry course was taught using traditional lecture methods, while students in another section were asked to problem solve in groups. The two sections were given the same final exam, and the grade distribution was similar in both sections. However, 33.3% of the students in the lecture section dropped the course, and only 17.3% of the students dropped the class in the section using cooperative learning. Moreover, the students who were asked to work in groups came to office hours more frequently and asked more questions in class.

Videos

The following are brief videos of examples of group work can be found on these sites:

Chasteen, S. (2010, June 29). Effective group work in college science class-rooms: Part 1 [YouTube video]. Retrieved from http://www.youtube.com/watch?v=TzMei8KDkGI

Chasteen, S. (2010, July 1). Effective group work in college science class-rooms: Part 2 [YouTube video]. Retrieved from http://www.youtube.com/watch?v=rUSN8vHRB-A

IDEA Papers

Barbara J. Millis provides a series of resources on learning in small groups in her IDEA papers:

Active learning strategies in face-to-face courses (IDEA Paper No. 53). (2012). Retrieved from Idea Center website: http://www.theideacenter.org/sites/default/files/paperidea_53.pdf

Enhancing learning—and more!—through cooperative learning (IDEA Paper No. 38). (2002). Retrieved from Idea Center website: http://www.theideacenter.org/sites/default/files/IDEA_Paper_38.pdf

Promoting deep learning (IDEA Paper No. 47). (2010). Retrieved from Idea Center website: http://www.theideacenter.org/sites/default/files/IDEA_Paper_47.pdf

---

Workshop 5.1
Problem-Based Learning

Complex, real-world problems are used to motivate students to identify and research the concepts and principles they need to know to work through those problems. Students work in small learning teams, bringing together collective skills at acquiring, communicating, and integrating information.

—Stanford University (n.d.)

We only think when we are confronted with problems.

—John Dewey (1906)

A PBL model is a type of group-oriented, engaged learning in which students participate in solving complex problems and work together to find a solution. Students who are working in small groups identify (a) what they already know about the topic, (b) what they need to know to solve the problem, and (c) what steps they will have to take to solve the problem. The instructor (known as the tutor in PBL) is responsible for enhancing learning by guiding students through the learning process (Schmidt, Rotgans, & Yew, 2011).

PBL encourages students to connect disciplinary knowledge to real-world problems— and in the process, motivates students to learn. Although it originated in medical schools, PBL is now also used widely in undergraduate education. The goals of PBL are to foster effective problem-solving and collaboration skills (Hmelo-Silver, 2004).

Studies have demonstrated that PBL boosts long-term retention of knowledge; increases library use, textbook reading, and class attendance; and promotes better study habits (Major & Palmer, 2001; Strobel & van Barneveld, 2009). PBL also encourages study- ing for meaning rather than simply memorizing facts. Strobel and van Barneveld (2009) found that PBL was more effective than traditional approaches for development of skills, long-term retention, and teacher and student satisfaction. Short-term retention was higher in students who studied using more traditional approaches.

Creating Problem-Based Learning Strategies Within Teams

The following list provides instructors with step-by-step guidelines for using PBL in their classes (Study Guides and Strategies, n.d.):

1. Give each team an "ill-structured" problem and ask them to discuss it. Having the team reach a consensus about the issues in each of the following steps is essential.
2. Create lists of what is known about the problem and what strengths and capabili- ties each team member has.
3. Create a written explanation of the problem based on the group's analysis of what is known and what is still needed to reach a solution.
4. List possible solutions, ordering them from strongest to weakest.
5. Choose the best solution.
6. List actions to be taken to solve the problem using a time line.
7. Create a list of what is still needed in order to solve the problem, as well as a list of possible resources. Determine if students will need to work individually or in teams to solve the problem. If the research supports the solution and if there is general agreement, go to step 8. If not, return to step 4.
8. Have teams write the solution with supporting documentation outside class and present their findings by summarizing the problem, the process, and the solution.
9. Review the performance.

Annotated Research Studies

Major, C. H., & Palmer, B. (2001). Assessing the effectiveness of problem-based learning in higher education: Lessons from the literature. *Academic Exchange Quarterly, 5*(1), 4–9.

According to this meta-analysis of students in the sciences, there is no significant difference between the knowledge acquired by PBL students and nonPBL students. However, students who learned by solving problems in PBL classrooms were more likely to transfer their knowledge to solve new and different problems. Moreover, PBL students were more likely to perceive that their communication skills, sense of responsibility, and critical-thinking skills were strong.

Strobel, J., & van Barneveld, A. (2009). When is PBL more effective? A meta-synthesis of meta-analyses comparing PBL to conventional classrooms. *Interdisciplinary Journal of Problem-Based Learning, 3*(1), 44–58.

This meta-analysis compared the effects of PBL to those of traditional forms of instruction. Although traditional approaches were more effective for students studying for short-term retention in standardized board exams, PBL was found to be more effective for long-term retention, skill development, class attendance, studying for meaning rather than recall, and satisfaction of students and teachers.

Videos

Short videos that demonstrate PBL classrooms can be found on YouTube:

Erasmus University. (2012, December 13). Erasmus University College—Problem based learning [YouTube video]. Retrieved from http://www.youtube.com/watch?v=ITjZqK_zhcl
Hoffman, C. (2011, February 16). Project-based learning explained by Westminster College [YouTube video]. Retrieved from http://www.youtube.com/watch?v=2KzWu8mQSZo

Online Resource

Bessant, S., Bailey, P., Robinson, Z., Tomkinson, C., Tomkinson, R., Ormerod, R., & Boast, R. (2013). *Problem-based learning: Case study of sustainability education: A toolkit for university educators.* Retrieved from http://www.heacademy.ac.uk/assets/documents/ntfs/Problem_Based_Learning_Toolkit.pdf

An online toolkit for introducing PBL in sustainability education.

Workshop 5.2
Process-Oriented Guided-Inquiry Learning

POGIL is a classroom and laboratory technique that seeks to simultaneously teach content and key process skills such as the ability to think analytically and work effectively as part of a collaborative team. Students work in small groups with individual roles to ensure that everyone is fully engaged in the learning process.

—POGIL Project (2013)

In POGIL students use class time to work in learning teams on specially designed activities. Students are divided into teams of three or four, and each student is assigned a role, such as manager, recorder, spokesperson, or reflector. During a POGIL activity, students are given a piece of data and then asked questions that require them to analyze that data. Once the students have drawn conclusions about their material, they are asked to apply this knowledge to a new situation. Students must reach consensus.

The group structure requires that students both listen to and learn from one another (POGIL Project, 2013). Students take on greater responsibility for their education; they learn to rely on thinking skills rather than memorization; they improve performance skills while learning subject content; and they develop positive relationships with other students and faculty (Hansen, 2006).

Annotated Research Studies

The POGIL Project website (www.pogil.org/about/effectiveness) summarizes the effectiveness of POGIL, citing the following research studies:

Farrell, J. J., Moog, R. S., & Spencer, J. N. (1999). A guided inquiry general chemistry course. *Journal of Chemical Education, 76*(4), 570–574. doi:10.1021/ed076p570

This study compares the performance of general chemistry students who were taught using traditional methods with those who were taught using the POGIL method over a 4-year period. The attrition rate for traditionally taught students was 21.9%. Fifty-two percent of those students who finished the course earned an A or B. The attrition rate for students taught using the POGIL method was only 9.6%, and 64% of those who finished the course earned an A or B.

Hanson, D. M., & Wolfskill, T. (2000). Process workshops—A new model for instruction. *Journal of Chemical Education, 77*(1), 120–130. doi:10.1021/ed077p120

Both high- and low-achieving students uniformly performed better on examinations after the implementation of the POGIL method in recitation sessions for general chemistry.

Lewis, J. E., & Lewis, S. E. (2005). Departing from lectures: An evaluation of a peer-led guided inquiry alternative. *Journal of Chemical Education, 82*(1), 135–139. doi:10.1021/ed082p135

Investigators analyzed the effect of replacing one of three general chemistry lectures each week with a POGIL session. Students who attended the team-learning sessions achieved above-average scores on the common examinations.

Straumanis, A., & Simons, E. A. (2008). A multi-institutional assessment of the use of POGIL in organic chemistry. In R. S. Moog & J. N. Spencer (Eds.), *Process-oriented guided inquiry learning* (pp. 224–237). New York, NY: Oxford University Press.

Complementary methods were used to compare POGIL and organic chemistry lecture courses in a multi-institutional study. The studies provide strong evidence of the effectiveness of POGIL. At each institution there were twice as many unsuccessful students in traditional sections as in POGIL sections.

Videos

Jensen, M. (2013). POGIL 01–07 [YouTube videos]. Retrieved from http://www.youtube.com/watch?v=OohcFS8CmXM&list=PLHfUqastpusvJBQmabvAcaiyD72EXRdm6&index=1

The following are brief videos demonstrating various aspects of a POGIL process:

POGIL Project. (2010, September 23). Pogil Web.mov [YouTube video]. Retrieved from http://www.youtube.com/watch?v=UkH1USXy8F0

A video demonstrating how POGIL works in a chemistry class at Franklin and Marshall College.

TED. (2011, January 10). Andrei Straumanis, TEDxSanMigueldeAllende [YouTube video]. Retrieved from http://www.youtube.com/watch?v=XFYVmJYGJe8

Andrei Straumanis presents a TED talk on POGIL.

Online Resource

POGIL Project, http://www.pogil.org/about

3

ASSESSMENT

Any time a learner tests out her ideas, she does it through action, and that action generates learning.

—James Zull (2002)

Without continuous assessment, student learning is limited to a one-shot, hit-or-miss event—maybe they get it, maybe they don't.

—Jay McTighe and Marcella Emberger (2006)

Chapter 3 focuses on assessment of learning. We share research that documents that students demonstrate higher achievement when frequent low-stakes formative assessment practices are implemented. In our workshops we also discuss summative assessment, or graded, high-stakes work that evaluates a student's competency at the end of a unit or the course. In addition we will examine assessment tools such as creating rubrics and developing grading practices.

Principle 6: Formative Assessment or Low-Stakes Evaluation Strengthens Retention

When the cook tastes the soup, that's formative; when the guests taste the soup, that's summative.

—Robert Stake (2004)

[Good assessment techniques make] your students review, retrieve, apply, analyze, synthesize or evaluate the material in your lectures, classroom activities, and reading assignments as well as their prior learning experiences.

—Linda Nilson (2010)

Formative assessment is a range of formal and informal evaluation strategies used by instructors to modify teaching and learning activities to improve retention (Shepard, 2005). These low-stakes evaluative strategies are based on the concept that when pressure to perform is minimal, students feel free to explore ideas or admit confusion. Formative assessment focuses on student learning early in the process, before the student receives a major grade (summative assessment), after which it may be more difficult to revise teaching and learning strategies. Additionally, formative assessments are effective for creating active lecture breaks, preparing students to engage in the material at the beginning of a class, or closing the day's class session.

Professors can help promote long-term recall by regularly asking students to apply and evaluate newly presented material. For example, after explaining a concept, an instructor can ask students to transfer this idea to a new situation. When instructors require students to put additional effort into organizing and retrieving information, they foster deeper learning (see Principle 1: Desirable Difficulties Increase Long-Term Retention, p. 5).

Recent research indicates that formative assessment may be more important than summative in terms of student learning. In two projects Black, Harrison, Lee, Marshall, and William (2003, 2004) determined that high-stakes grading tends to stress competition instead of personal improvement. Moreover, feedback from summative assessments can have an adverse effect on low-achieving students who believe that they lack ability and, therefore, cannot learn. Feedback from a final exam may not be provided or may be offered too late to improve learning. However, student achievement increases with the use of practice testing or repeated retrieval and other formative assessment techniques (Black et al., 2003).

In fact, Karpicke and Roediger (2007) found "repeated retrieval to be the key to enhancing later retention" (p. 159). Practice testing does not have to be complicated or a time-consuming in-class activity: students can answer questions at the end of a lecture or take online quizzes outside class time. However, according to recent studies, to fully benefit from practice testing, students need to take these assessments during different sessions over time. The longer the intervals between practice sessions the greater the benefits (Carpenter, Pashler, & Cepeda, 2009; Rohrer, 2009; Rohrer & Taylor, 2006). (See Principle 2: Meaningful and Spaced Repetition Increases Retention, p. 12.)

Studies also indicate that both writing better test questions and asking better questions in class result in deeper learning (Anderson & Krathwohl, 2001; Black et al., 2003, 2004). Lower-level questions deal solely with recalling and remembering (Bloom, 1956), whereas higher-level questions involve evaluating and creating. Bloom (1956) designed a tiered model of classifying thinking and questioning, which was later revised by Anderson and Krathwohl (2001). This hierarchy can apply to both formative and summative assessments.

The categories of Bloom's revised taxonomy (Anderson & Krathwohl, 2001), with examples of key verbs, are as follows:

- Remembering (lowest level): Recalling, defining, listing, describing
- Understanding: Interpreting, summarizing, inferring, paraphrasing, classifying
- Applying: Implementing, using, executing
- Analyzing: Comparing, organizing, deconstructing, attributing, outlining
- Evaluating: Checking, critiquing, judging, testing
- Creating (highest level): Designing, constructing, planning, producing

Asking strong questions in class is a basic formative assessment strategy to assess retention, understanding, and application. Nilson (2010) suggests opening a discussion with a few *remembering*-stage questions (who, what, where, and when) as a mental warm-up, although she cautions instructors to avoid questions that call for one- or two-word answers. Follow these questions by moving to the *understanding* stage, which checks for comprehension and allows time to clarify misconceptions. Students should then be ready to respond to *application* questions, which require problem solving. Finally, they can *evaluate*, or critique, the strengths and shortcomings of the argument and then *create* their own model. (See also Appendix C, "Workshop on Classroom Discussions," p. 73.)

Following are a few resources for creating learning objectives, teaching strategies, and sample questions using Bloom's revised taxonomy:

Educational Origami. (n.d.). Bloom's digital taxonomy. Retrieved from http://edorigami.wikispaces.com/Bloom%27s+Digital+Taxonomy
Iowa State University, Center for Learning and Teaching. (2011). A model of learning objectives. Retrieved from http://www.celt.iastate.edu/teaching/Revised-Blooms1.html
University of North Carolina–Charlotte, Center for Teaching and Learning. (2004). Writing objectives using Bloom's taxonomy. Retrieved from http://teaching.uncc.edu/articles-books/best-practice-articles/goals-objectives/writing-objectives-using-blooms-taxonomy

Effective formative assessment must be coupled with feedback that provides information to help students progress to meet established criteria. This feedback is balanced between reinforcing positive attributes that should be maintained and constructive feedback indicating what should be modified. Feedback should be offered frequently and given to both individual students and the class. Peer feedback may also be valuable when used with a rubric or with clear guidance about how to assess and be constructive with one's classmates.

Instructional Applications

Minute Paper or Muddiest Point
In the last 5 or 10 minutes of class, ask students to write either the most important thing learned in the day's class or one to two important questions about the lecture or reading assignment. These responses can be used to start the next class in order to connect discussions between days and can also motivate students to be punctual.

Just-in-Time Teaching
Just-in-Time Teaching (JiTT) asks students to respond to web-based questions that they receive before class as warm-up exercises (Novak, Patterson, Gavrin, Christian, & Forinash, 1999). Two questions usually focus on key principles with the third question addressing more open-ended topics. Answers are due before class begins. The instructor reviews student responses and develops classroom activities based on the trouble spots.

Note Sharing
Periodically pause for a few moments and allow groups of two to three students to compare notes. This allows the students to write down information they may have missed and double-check to see that they understand the most important points in the lecture.

Student-Created Flash Cards
Ask students to create their own flash cards to test themselves and others when working in small groups. Websites and apps—such as Evernote Peek (http://evernote.com/peek), Study Blue (www.studyblue.com/study-tools), and Flashcard Machine (www.flashcardmachine.com)—are also available to create digital flash cards on computers, tablets, and cell phones.

Think-Pair-Share
This strategy can serve as an excellent in-class questioning technique to encourage discussion and to assess learning. Students reflect on a question (think), discuss possible answers with another student (pair), and share responses with the class (share) (see p. 34). Think-pair-share can alternately

be presented as "think-pair-scare," with the "scare" being a quiz. Variations on this strategy include asking students to reach a consensus, which they either turn in or share with the class.

Pre- and Post-Assessment

Devise questions for students to answer at the beginning of the unit (or class) that will inform instructors about student knowledge and skill level as well as reveal their underlying assumptions about the material. Ask the same questions at the end of the unit so that student and instructor alike can determine how their knowledge and perceptions have changed.

Scratch-Off Sheets

The immediate feedback assessment technique (IF-AT) uses a multiple-choice form much like a lottery ticket. Students scratch off their answer to a question on the form. If the response is correct, a star appears within the scratched-off rectangle. Students can also work in small groups to come to a consensus on the correct answer. (For more information about IF-AT, see www.epsteineducation.com/home/about/.)

Background Knowledge Probe

Students' prior knowledge can be evaluated on the first day of class or before introducing a new unit by using a few short-answer or multiple-choice questions. In the next class, share the results with students and explain how their current knowledge can affect them as learners.

Knowledge Survey

Instead of asking students to answer questions, a knowledge survey measures students' confidence in their ability to answer questions accurately. The Cornell University Center for Teaching Excellence provides a valuable website on knowledge surveys (see Cornell University, 2013).

Misconception/Preconception Check

Checking student misconceptions or preconceptions is useful in classes that deal with potentially contentious or sensitive material. Create a brief questionnaire to determine problematic assumptions that may interfere with student learning.

Pick Your Poison

Ask students to write test questions for their next exam. Share the questions with the class. Let students know the best questions will be included on the next exam.

Peer- and Self-Assessment

For group assignments, ask students to complete and submit a confidential form used to assess how well they and other members of their group met particular expectations (that are clearly noted in the assignment). Examples include meeting deadlines, providing feedback, and dividing the workload. The information provided does not have to be part of the students' grades, but be sure to give out these forms at the start of the project in order to preempt common problems that can arise during group work, such as poor division of labor.

What You Know, What You Want to Know, and What You Learned

A "what you know, what you want to know, and what you learned" (KWL) chart helps activate prior knowledge and prime the pump for student learning. The chart has three columns. Before beginning a reading assignment, the students fill out the first two columns of the chart (*K*, for what the students already know, and *W*, for what the students want to know). After reading the assignment, students fill in the third column, *L*, for what they learned on completion of the assignment. A fourth column, *C*, can be added to address what students still find confusing (KWLC). The KWL(C) chart both motivates students and gives the instructor insight into students' prior and developing knowledge (University of Illinois Online Network, n.d.).

Classroom Response Systems

Use electronic classroom response systems, such as iClickers, or the students' own smartphones to assess how well students understand the reading at the beginning of class or the material discussed at the middle or end of class. For more information about classroom response systems, see *Agile Learning* (http://derekbruff.org/?cat=122).

Low-Tech Clickers

Create large flash cards by folding a piece of paper into four quadrants, each with a unique color or letter that corresponds to an answer to a question. Students are instructed to answer a question by displaying the appropriate color or letter under their chin. This allows the instructor to quickly scan the room to assess understanding of the concept. As a simple alternative, students can display 1, 2, 3, or 4 fingers under their chin to correspond to A, B, C, or D of a multiple-choice question.

Four-Question Technique

Dietz-Uhler and Lanter (2009) found students' quiz scores improved when they were asked the following four questions about an in-class activity:

1. What is one important concept, research finding, theory, or idea in psychology that you learned while completing this activity?
2. Why do you believe that this concept, research finding, theory, or idea in psychology is important?
3. Can you apply what you have learned from this activity to some aspect of your life?
4. What question(s) has the activity raised for you, and what are you still wondering about?

Waiting for an Answer

While not a specific assessment technique, waiting for an answer after posing a question can strengthen the assessment process. Given time to think about their response, students can better formulate answers. In addition, they are more likely to participate in classroom discussions when given adequate time to think about responses.

ConcepTests

Eric Mazur (1997) developed ConcepTests to introduce active-learning strategies into a physics lecture without having to significantly restructure his classes. These tests, a variation of think-pair-share, ask students to individually answer multiple-choice questions. After they have formulated their answers, students work in groups following a protocol that can be adapted to the needs of the professor. For further details and videos, see McConnell (2012).

Critical Incident Questionnaire

A critical incident questionnaire (CIQ) is a one-page form distributed to students at the end of class each week. It is composed of five questions asking students to recall details about events that happened in the class that week. The CIQ encourages students to focus on specific, concrete discussions and events. For more information about CIQs, see Brookfield (2013).

Annotated Research Studies

Gier, V. S., & Kriener, D. S. (2009). Incorporating active learning with Power-Point–based lectures using content-based questions. *Teaching of Psychology, 36*(2), 134–139.

An experimental group of psychology students received handouts of slides from PowerPoint lectures plus practice test questions generated from these presentations. The control group, a second section of the same class taught by the same instructor, received the PowerPoint lecture slides and the hand-outs and then met in small groups for 30-minute discussions but were not provided the practice test questions. Results indicated that the experimental group with the practice test questions performed significantly better on the unit and final exams than the control group.

Higgins, R., Hartley, P., & Skelton, P. (2002). The conscientious consumer: Reconsidering the role of assessment feedback in student learning. *Studies in Higher Education, 27*(1), 53–64.

This article reports the findings of a 3-year research project that investigated the impact of student assessment and feedback in higher education. Findings indicated that formative assessment feedback was key in students' learning deeply.

Karpicke, J., & Blunt, J. (2011). Retrieval practice produces more learning than elaborative studying with concept mapping. *Science, 331*(6018), 772–775. doi:10.1126/science.1199327

This study involving 200 college students found that taking a practice test before an exam better prepared students than other methods of studying—including repetition and concept mapping. Students were divided into four groups and asked to read several paragraphs about a scientific topic. Each group performed one of the following learning strategies: (a) reading the text for 5 minutes, (b) reading the text in four consecutive 5-minute sessions, (c) drawing diagrams about information from the excerpt they were reading, and (d) reading the passage once and taking a "retrieval practice test" that required them to write down what they recalled. A week later all four groups took a quiz asking them to recall facts from the passage they had read and to draw conclusions on the basis of those facts. Students in the fourth group, who took the practice test, recalled 50% more of the material than those in the other three groups. Investigators concluded that by organizing and creating meaningful connections, struggling to remember information, and identifying areas of weakness, students were able to better recall information.

Lyle, K. B., & Crawford, N. A. (2011). Retrieving essential material at the end of lectures improves performance on statistics exams. *Teaching of Psychology, 38*(2), 94–97.

The authors explored what they call the PUREMEM (pronounced "pure mem," pure memory, or practicing unassisted retrieval to enhance memory for essential material) technique. They found that students had higher exam scores when they were asked to respond to questions on new material at the end of their stats class. Exam scores were significantly higher in the course section that was taught using the PUREMEM strategies than in the section taught without them.

McDaniel, M. A., Howard, D. C., & Einstein, G. O. (2009). The read-recite-review study strategy: Effective and portable. *Psychological Science, 20*(4), 516–522.

Two groups of engineering students were tested on recall of reading materials immediately and then again after a one-week delay. The first group reviewed the material by taking multiple-choice and short-answer practice tests. The second group reread the material and took notes on the information. The members of the first group, who had taken the practice tests, performed better both immediately and after the one-week delay.

McDaniel, M. A., Wildman, K. M., & Anderson, J. L. (2012). Using quizzes to enhance summative-assessment performance in a web-based class: An experimental study. *Journal of Applied Research in Memory and Cognition, 1*, 18–26.

In a web-based college class, core concepts were quizzed in practice tests with multiple-choice and short-answer questions, while other concepts were not. Multiple attempts on each practice test were encouraged, and feedback was available after each. The practice tests enhanced exam performance significantly when the questions were worded identically but also nominally when worded differently.

Roediger, H. L., Agarwal, P. K., McDaniel, M. A., & McDermott, K. B. (2011). Test-enhanced learning in the classroom: Long-term benefits from quizzing. *Journal of Experimental Psychology: Applied, 17*(4), 382–395. doi:10.1037/a0026252

The authors incorporated online practice tests into a cognitive psychology undergraduate lecture course. With the addition of these tests to the course, class performance improved according to several criteria relative to prior semesters when practice tests were not used. Practice tests were found to be a practical way to help students learn and retain the course material, without taking class time.

Videos

Western Washington University, Center for Instructional Innovation. (2008, April 17). Using assessment to improve instruction [YouTube video]. Retrieved from http://www.youtube.com/watch?v=BZ3USs16J3Y

Xeriland, T. (2012, March 12). Formative assessment/evaluation [YouTube video]. Retrieved from http://www.youtube.com/watch?v=cvXS2x3UhQU

Workshop 6.1
Grading, Summative Assessment, and High-Stakes Evaluation

Let us not judge our students simply on what they know.
Rather let them be judged on what they can generate
from what they know—how well they can leap
the barrier from learning to thinking.

—Jerome Bruner (1961)

Feedback or knowledge of results is the lifeblood of learning.

—Derek Rowntree (1987)

Summative assessments are recorded judgments about student performance. Techniques for summative assessment include papers, exams, portfolios, projects, laboratory notebooks, artistic performances, in-class demonstrations, journals, homework, problem sets, reports, clinical experiences, research projects, case studies, posters, and exhibits. Some of these techniques can also be used as formative or low-stakes assessment, but the focus in this workshop is on summative assessment. Instructors are encouraged to vary their assessment strategies, allowing students to demonstrate learning in multiple ways over time (Wiggins & McTighe, 2005).

When considering summative assessment strategies, Wiggins and McTighe (2005) advocate backward design or planning the learning outcomes before developing assessment techniques. The backward design model focuses on beginning the planning process by identifying the results desired at the end of the course. The instructor then works backward "to develop instruction rather than the traditional approach, which begins with defining what topics need to be covered" (Wiggins, 2005) and creating a syllabus from these topics.

As instructors are planning evaluation of learning in a course, Wiggins and McTighe (2005, p. 146) encourage them to consider the following:

1. What do they want students to learn by the conclusion of this course?
2. What would count as evidence of successful learning?
3. What specific characteristics in student responses, products, or performances demonstrate successful learning?
4. Do results give a clear picture of the students' understanding of the course goals?

Assessments of learning should be made early and often and should include both formative and summative assessments to give students more feedback about their learning. Myers and Myers (2007) compared two sections of statistics with the same content and instructor. The control group had only a midterm and final, whereas the experimental section had biweekly exams and the same final. At the end of the semester, the experimental section, which received regular feedback via multiple summative assessments throughout the semester, scored 15% higher on the final exam. Moreover, this group had significantly fewer withdrawals and ranked the course and instructor significantly higher than the control group did.

Workshop 6.1A
Creating Assessment Tools

Developing criteria for assessment can do the following:

- Help determine what to teach and how to teach it
- Communicate early expectations to students about how their work will be evaluated
- Save the instructor time
- Make grading more uniform and fair

To minimize student confusion about grades remember the following:

- Include grading policies and procedures in your syllabus (see Workshop A.1: The Syllabus, p. 61)
- Remind students of grading criteria when both assigning work and returning graded work
- Minimize in-class discussion of grades and instead concentrate on the course's learning objectives (Vanderbilt University, n.d.)

Writing Test Questions

Ideally, some of the test questions will be written before the course begins while determining what students need to learn and what evidence will be needed to demonstrate knowledge has been attained. Include both formative and summative assessments when planning courses. Most formative preparatory assignments, quizzes, or homework may be ungraded, pass/fail, or check/check-plus (see Principle 6: Formative Assessment or Low-Stakes Evaluation Strengthens Retention, p. 43).

Immediately after teaching material in class, review the test questions created before the course began. This is an excellent time to edit previously designed questions for clarity and emphasis. Then write additional questions based on recent instruction and course objectives. Consider including a variety of types of questions based on course objectives, such as true/false, matching, multiple-choice, fill-in-the-blank, and essay questions. In addition to assessing factual information, multiple-choice test questions can also assess higher-order thinking skills (Bloom, 1956; see the categories of Bloom's revised taxonomy, p. 45) if based on a realistic stimulus, such as a new scenario, table, graph, or quotation. The following are excellent resources about creating multiple-choice questions:

Brigham Young University, Faculty Center. (2001). 14 rules for writing multiple-choice questions. Retrieved from http://testing.byu.edu/info/handbooks/14%20Rules%20 for%20Writing%20Multiple-Choice%20Questions.pdf

Burton, S. J., Sudweeks, R. R., Merrill, P. F., & Wood, B. (1991). *How to prepare better multiple-choice test items: Guidelines for university faculty*. Retrieved from Brigham

Young University Testing Center website: http://testing.byu.edu/info/handbooks/betteritems.pdf

Vanderbilt University, Center for Teaching. (n.d.). Writing good multiple choice test questions. Retrieved from http://cft.vanderbilt.edu/teaching-guides/assessment/writing-good-multiple-choice-test-questions/

Using Portfolio Assessments

When using student portfolios for assessment purposes, remember the following:

- Student portfolios are collections of their work that represent their progress in a class or program.
- Examples of students' work can show their range of skills and abilities and can be used to show development and growth.
- Effective portfolios can be electronic or hard copy.

Online Resources

Bruff, D. (2009–2010). Multiple-choice questions you wouldn't put on a test: Promoting deep learning using clickers. *Essays on Teaching Excellence, 21*(3). Retrieved from http://podnetwork.org/content/uploads/V21-N3-Bruff.pdf

Harvard University, Derek Bok Center for Teaching and Learning. (2006). Grading papers. Retrieved from http://isites.harvard.edu/fs/html/icb.topic58474/GradingPapers.html

Jacobs, L. (n.d.). *How to write better tests: A handbook for improving test construction skills.* Retrieved from Indiana University–Bloomington website: http://www.indiana.edu/~best/pdf_docs/better_tests.pdf

Reiner, C., Bothell, T., Sudweeks, R., & Wood, B. (2002). *Preparing effective essay questions: A self-directed workbook for educators.* Stillwater, OK: New Forums Press. Retrieved from Brigham Young University Testing Center website: http://testing.byu.edu/info/handbooks/WritingEffectiveEssayQuestions.pdf

Teaching Effectiveness Program. (2013, May 16). Writing multiple-choice questions that demand critical thinking. Retrieved from University of Oregon Teaching and Learning Center website: http://tep.uoregon.edu/resources/assessment/multiplechoicequestions/mc4critthink.html

University of Washington, Center for Teaching and Learning. (n.d.). Constructing tests: Essay questions. Retrieved from http://www.washington.edu/teaching/constructing-tests/#essayquestions

Vanderbilt University, Center for Teaching. (n.d.). Grading student work. Retrieved from http://cft.vanderbilt.edu/teaching-guides/assessment/grading-student-work/

Workshop 6.1B
Constructing Rubrics

One way to measure student performance against a predetermined set of criteria is to create a rubric—a scoring scale that contains criteria for a task and appropriate levels of performance. "A rubric allows for standardized evaluation according to specified criteria to make evaluating simpler and more transparent in a reliable, fair, and valid manner. It can give students clear feedback about their performance" (Kappa Omicron Nu Honor Society, 2013). A rubric can also save the instructor time in grading. While it is a summative assessment, it can also be used as a formative assessment during revision of a project or document (Mueller, 2012).

An online tutorial for creating a rubric is available from University of Colorado–Denver (2006). This resource presents a step-by-step process for creating rubrics, criteria for judging rubrics, and examples of different types of rubrics.

Steps for Developing a Rubric

When developing effective rubrics, instructors are encouraged to consider the following steps (University of Colorado–Denver, 2006):

1. Determine the purpose of the assignment and what students should learn. Will students receive a grade based on the rubric, or will the feedback be formative only?
2. Determine what type of rubric will be created. An analytic rubric breaks down a complex project into individual components with each skill or component scored separately. A holistic rubric, on the other hand, is used to make an overall judgment on a minor assignment with feedback about a learning task with a single score.
3. Create criteria for the project by determining what students should learn from the task. How will they demonstrate that they have learned the task? What are characteristics of the final product? Are the criteria observable and measurable?
4. Design the rating scale for the rubric. A 2-point, or all-or-nothing, checklist simply indicates whether the project met or did not meet standards. To provide more detailed feedback, use a 4- or 5-point rating scale.
5. Write performance descriptors for each scale point. These descriptors should be observable and measurable behaviors, should use parallel language with each point, and should indicate the degree to which standards are met.
6. Double-check the new rubric for consistency and effective assessment of the task. After using the rubric with student projects, refine it to make it even more effective.

Undergraduate Research Paper Rubric

Undergraduate research is becoming more important in higher education. Clear, inquiry-based learning and scholarship promote student learning. The standards listed in Table 3.1 describe effective research papers.

TABLE 3.1
Rubric for Evaluating Undergraduate Research Papers

Standards	5–4 Exemplary	3–2 Satisfactory	1–0 Unacceptable	Score	Weight	Total Score
Abstract	Clearly states problem and question to be resolved; clearly summarizes method, results, and conclusions	Summarizes problem, method, results, and conclusions but lacks some details	Is vague about the problem; does not provide a summary of the whole project		X 2	
Introduction	Provides background research on the topic and summarizes important findings from the review of the literature; describes problem to be solved; justifies the study; explains the significance of the problem to an audience of nonspecialists	Provides background research into the topic and describes the problem to be solved	Provides background research on the topic but does not describe the problem to be solved; insufficient or nonexistent explanation of details for nonspecialists		X 1	
Discussion	Addresses the topic with clarity; organizes and synthesizes information; draws conclusions	Addresses the topic; lacks substantive conclusions; sometimes digresses from topic of focus	Presents little to no clarity in formulating conclusions or organization		X 2	
Summary	Presents clear recommendations or implications for future research	Presents a logical explanation for findings	Does not adequately explain findings		X 2	
Mechanics and Documentation	Examines paper for accuracy of grammar, spelling, and writing mechanics; compares text with documentation to ensure accuracy of sources	Demonstrates an understanding of grammar, spelling, writing mechanics, and appropriate documentation.	Has errors that obscure meaning of content or add confusion; neglects important sources or documents few to no resources		X 1	

Note. We gratefully acknowledge permission to share this rubric, created by Dorothy I. Mitstifer, Kappa Omicron Nu Honor Society, www.kon.org/contact.html.

Online Resources

General Education Critical Thinking Rubric (Northeastern Illinois University), http://cft
  .vanderbilt.edu/files/Rubric-Critical-Thinking-NE-Illinois.pdf

Georgia State University, Center for Instructional Innovation, http://cii.gsu.edu/writing-
  across-the-curriculum/resources/assignments-syllabi-rubrics/

Indiana University–Purdue University Indianapolis, https://sites.google.com/site/iupuinca
  2012/Home/creating-rubrics

iRubric, http://www.rcampus.com/indexrubric.cfm

National Institute for Learning Outcomes Assessment, http://www.learningoutcomeassess
  ment.org/Rubrics.htm

Rubric for Opinion Paper (Derek Bruff), http://cft.vanderbilt.edu/files/Rubric-Opinion-
  Paper-DB.pdf

Rubric for Research Paper (Winona State), http://cft.vanderbilt.edu/files/Rubric-Research-
  Paper-Winona-State.pdf

Rubric Samples for Higher Education (Kappa Omicron Nu Honor Society). http://rubrics
  .kappaomicronnu.org/contact.html

Valid Assessment of Learning in Undergraduate Education (VALUE), http://www.aacu.org/
  value/rubrics/index_p.cfm?CFID=47221224&CFTOKEN=21204686

Workshop 6.1C
Tips for Grading Papers and Essay Exams

The following suggestions may be helpful when reading essays and grading papers:

Create assignments that have well-defined objectives for assessment so students understand what they are asked to do.

Grade in a pleasant place, free from distraction. If grading is a semipleasant activity done in comfortable surroundings, it will not be quite as painful.

Read 5 or 10 papers or exams before making any marks at all. Assign preliminary grades on sticky notes. Place these notes in order from best to worst and determine grading scheme from there.

Establish a grading schedule. Determine an overall schedule and set a timer for each paper. Use a time limit as an average because some papers and exams may take longer than others. Grade no more than 20 pieces of student work at a time to avoid burnout and lack of attention to detail.

Put potentially plagiarized papers in a pile and check them all at once. Checking for plagiarism can be time consuming. Put suspicious papers in a pile to be examined later. When dealing with these papers, check Google or Google Scholar first. Take the oddest phrase and put it in quotes.

Restrict comments to those that students can use for future improvement. Spend more time on providing guidance for students for future work rather than on grading itself.

Devote time to important issues—such as the thesis statement and the paper's strengths and weaknesses—first. Final comments should prompt further inquiry by students instead of providing them with answers (Vanderbilt University, n.d.).

Do not correct grammar/spelling on each page. Trying to fix mistakes or to highlight the errors on each page can be time consuming. Circle and fix offending words in the first paragraph or on the first page. Then write a note in the margin encouraging the student to make similar changes in the paper and resubmit. Students do not tend to learn from comments made on written work after they have completed the paper and have received a grade (Semke, 1984).

Have students give feedback to each other. This practice will save the instructor time commenting on mistakes that could have been caught by a peer. A rubric can be particularly helpful when peer editing as students may initially be reluctant to give less than positive feedback to a peer.

Don't waste time on careless student work. Ask students to complete a checklist and attach it to their papers before submission for grading. Items on the checklist could include revising, proofreading, and asking for peer feedback. This checklist can serve as a good reminder that basic issues should be addressed before a student submits a paper (Walvoord & Anderson, 1998).

Provide students with a guide for grading. Shaw (1984), for example, states that students should know that if they can answer no to any of the following four questions, the grade for their paper will be lowered significantly:

- Does the paper have a thesis?
- Does the thesis address itself to an appropriate question or topic?
- Is the paper free from long stretches of quotations and summaries that exist only for their own sakes and remain unanalyzed?
- Is the paper largely free of basic grammatical errors?

Ask students to correct their tests (perhaps to increase their grade) so that they can learn from their mistakes. Allowing test corrections may save time grading because the professor need give only a little feedback for wrong answers. The corrections may not take much time to grade since there is a higher likelihood that the answers will be mostly correct.

Provide video feedback on grading. Personalized feedback using video can also be helpful. It can be more personal to view an instructor discussing a paper rather than reading notes in the margin. It can also save the instructor time. Instructors can take a digital picture of a student paper, convert it to a PDF, write comments on it, and then record a video with verbal comments. Before meeting with students, ask them to view their personalized feedback video. Several apps are available to create these videos, including ScreenChomp (www.techsmith.com/screenchomp.html) and Camtasia (www.techsmith .com/camtasia.html). A short explanatory video is available on YouTube:

Spencer, D. (2012, March 30). Personalized feedback with ScreenChomp [YouTube video.] Retrieved from http://www.youtube.com/watch?v=igp7rHZRg4M&feature=youtu.be

Workshop 6.2
Soliciting Midsemester Student Feedback to Improve a Course

While knowing thyself is useful, it's also useful to
know what your students are thinking.

—Brian Croxall (2012)

Instructors are encouraged to solicit student feedback about the course during the semester. This process can either be informal and individual or involve the institution's teaching center. Students take more seriously the opportunity to give their instructors midterm feedback than they do opportunities for end-of-the-semester feedback because they stand to benefit more from the earlier requests (Nilson, 2010). Instructors then have the opportunity to explain why they are making some requested changes and not others. Instructors who provide reasons for their decisions demonstrate that they are listening to student concerns and can often make a difference in class climate and the learning environment (Lewis, 2001). (See Principle 3: Emotion and Relevance Deepen Learning, p. 15.) Moreover, research has found that these evaluations have resulted in significantly higher student evaluations at the end of the term (Cohen, 1980).

Instructional Applications

Midcourse Evaluation
After the fourth or fifth week of classes, ask students what is working and what improvements need to be made in the course to help them learn more effectively. The response rate will be higher if this evaluation takes place during class. Of course, these student evaluations should be anonymous. Students will be able to provide better feedback if they have specific questions to answer, for example, "What do you think is going well in this course?" or "What changes would you like to see to facilitate your learning?" After reading the evaluations, summarize them for the students and discuss plans for implementing or not implementing their suggestions. Finally, talking with a colleague about these evaluations can also be helpful and can provide another perspective.

Small-Group Instructional Diagnosis
Small-group instructional diagnosis (SGID) "generates feedback from midterm small-group discussion among students about a course. Students offer suggestions to solving problems in instruction for the instructor's consideration" (Clark & Redmond, 1982, p. 2). This technique allows the instructor to gather impartial feedback from students. SGIDs are most effective if they are conducted before the middle of the semester, allowing the instructor time to make necessary changes. This process requires asking a facilitator to meet with students to collect honest feedback. Teaching and learning centers can be an excellent resource, but colleagues from outside the department or institution can also serve as

outside interviewers. The interviewer should divide students into groups and ask groups to respond to questions such as, What is working in the class? What is not working? What suggestions can be offered to improve the class? The outsider then polls the group as a whole and focuses on consensus and solutions rather than concerns (Cook-Sather, 2009; Sorenson, 2001). Later, the facilitator discusses students' suggestions and concerns with the professor. However, for this protocol to work, students must be assured that their anonymity will be preserved.

Public Midterm Evaluations Using Google Docs

Midsemester, Croxall (2012) modified settings in a Google doc to allow students to edit the document and view one another's edits. He then asked them to respond anonymously to two brief prompts in the document in class: "What is working?" and "What could be done better?" He wanted students to know what their peers thought were strengths and weaknesses of the class. Because the comments were "public," the students could then hold him accountable to respond to them. Croxall also found that students wrote more in response to open-ended questions when they could use a keyboard than when they had to write by hand.

Focus/Advisory Groups

In a large class, the instructor meets every few weeks with 6–10 randomly chosen students to talk about how the course is going. Do more listening than talking in these meetings. Some colleges and universities have teaching and learning centers that can facilitate these meetings.

Appendix A

COURSE DESIGN WORKSHOPS

Workshop A.1
The Syllabus

*If you don't know where you are goin',
you will probably not wind up there.*
—Forrest Gump, *Gumpisms* (Groom, 1994)

*A syllabus can be many things, but faculty should not neglect its
power to communicate important messages and motivate and
set high standards. In addition to serving as a contract with
students and a way to clarify goals of the course, a syllabus
is students' first contact with you and the course material.*
—José Bowen (2012)

The syllabus may be the first statement that students encounter in a class. It gives students a message not only about the professor but also about the goals of the course. For example, when Ken Bain (2004), author of *What the Best College Teachers Do*, is planning a syllabus, he asks himself the following questions:

- What big questions will my course help students answer?
- What skills, abilities, or qualities will my course help them develop?
- How will I encourage my students' interest in these questions and abilities?
- What reasoning abilities must students have or develop to answer the questions that the course raises?
- What mental models are students likely to bring with them that I will want them to challenge?
- What information will my students need to understand in order to answer the important question of the course? How will they best obtain that information?

- How will I share the intellectual and professional standards I will be using in assessing students' work? Why do I use those standards? How will I help students learn to assess their own work using those standards?

Bain develops his syllabus from the answers to these questions. Instead of designing a syllabus solely around content topics, he uses the syllabus as a tool to determine how he can achieve his course goals.

Bain's questions are congruent with Wiggins and McTighe's (2005) method of backward design. They advocate creating a syllabus, as well as a course, in three phases, using the following backward design process:

1. Identify desired results. At the end of the term, what should students know, understand, and be able to do?
2. Determine assessment evidence. What projects or other assessment methods will be used for students to demonstrate their progress in meeting learning objectives?
3. Plan learning experiences and instruction. What assignments, questions, and strategies will be used to help students develop their abilities?

Whether or not an instructor chooses to use backward design, it is important to create a thoughtful syllabus. Recently, educators have begun to focus not only on the information conveyed in a syllabus but also on the tone of the information communicated. Harnish et al. (2011) define a *warm syllabus* as one that "removes unnecessary and unhelpful barriers between instructors and students, making the classroom a comfortable and safe place for discovery." Wasley (2008b) notes that in classes with syllabi with a less punitive tone—for example, those with fewer bolded statements with exclamation points regarding consequences—students are more likely to approach their professor. In "Creating the Foundation for a Warm Classroom Climate," Harnish et al. (2011) include the following components for a positive tone that may help build class community:

- Positive or friendly language
- Rationale for assignments
- Humor
- Compassion (While instructors should have clear policies, they may want to acknowledge that unforeseen events do occur.)
- Enthusiasm for the topic

In fact, Singham (2007) and Wasley (2008b) advocate abandoning the traditional, rule-laden syllabus for a less legalistic and more learner-friendly syllabus. Singham (2007) goes so far as to advocate that students build their own syllabus. He suggests that professors go to class the first day with a tentative time line for reading and writing assignments. When students and professors know one another better, they discuss and decide together the criteria for a good paper, define good participation, and create rubrics for assessing student performance. In Singham's experience, the students are more invested in the class when they collaborate on developing the syllabus.

To create a thoughtful and effective syllabus, instructors should include the following components (Lowther, Stark, & Martens, 1989; Nilson, 2010, pp. 33–36):

- Instructor contact information, office hours, and communication information, such as Twitter, e-mail response time, and network requests
- Course requirements, grading scale, and criteria
- Required and optional materials
- Course purpose and learning outcomes
- Policies on attendance and missed or late assignments
- Academic integrity policy
- Organization of the course with calendar
- Statement that the syllabus may be subject to change by mutual agreement

Syllabi are frequently reviewed in the promotion and tenure process. Instructors are encouraged to check with their institutions on the role the syllabi will play in assessment processes.

Annotated Resources

Fink, L. D. (2005, August). *A self-directed guide to designing courses for significant learning.* Retrieved from http://www.deefinkandassociates.com/GuidetoCourseDesignAug05 .pdf

This brief free online workbook helps instructors design courses that include such components as active learning, significant learning, and educative assessment.

Fink, L. D. (2013). *Creating significant learning experiences: An integrated approach to designing college courses* (Rev. ed.). San Francisco, CA: Jossey-Bass.

This newly updated edition helps instructors with the design process. It combines current research-based practices with learning-centered strategies. The author asks educators to think about learning objectives and to create learning strategies that maximize student achievement.

Harnish, R., McElwee, R., Slattery, J., Frantz, S., Haney, M., Shore, C., & Penley, J. (2011). Creating the foundation for a warm classroom climate: Best practices in syllabus tone. *Observer, 24*(1). Retrieved from http://www.psychologicalscience.org/index.php/ publications/observer/2011/january-11/creating-the-foundation-for-a-warm-classroom-climate.html

This article discusses the implications and importance the syllabus has on creating tone in the classroom and lists ideas that instructors might implement to help create a warm classroom climate.

Hara, B. (2010, October 19). Graphic display of student learning objectives [web log post]. *ProfHacker.* Retrieved from http://chronicle.com/blogs/profhacker/graphic-display-of-student-learning-objectives/27863

Hara shares three examples of graphic displays of course objectives used in syllabi.

Nilson, L. B. (2007). *The graphic syllabus and the outcomes map: Communicating your course.* San Francisco, CA: Jossey-Bass.

Nilson advocates creating a graphic syllabus and an outcomes map, which may look like a diagram, flow chart, or concept map. The strength of a graphic syllabus is that it can show relationships among topics and the learning process to achieve understanding of those topics.

O'Brien, J. G., Millis, B. J., & Cohen, M. W. (2008). *The course syllabus: A learning centered approach* (2nd ed.). San Francisco, CA: Jossey-Bass.

The authors present eight principles for designing a course that promote critical thinking. The book also advocates changing the focus of the syllabus from material to be covered to student learning tools.

Slattery, J. M., & Carlson, J. (2005). Preparing an effective syllabus: Current best practices. *College Teaching, 53*(4), 159–164.

This article suggests that the tone of a syllabus (friendly or punitive) sets the tone for class and cites studies that indicate students perform better in classrooms where there is a friendly tone. The authors also suggest that a syllabus should be the product of a strongly articulated teaching philosophy.

Wasley, P. (2008a). Research yields tips on crafting better syllabi. *Chronicle of Higher Education, 54*(27), A11–A12.

This article reviews several studies on the relationship between the tone of a syllabus and student engagement. The findings indicate that students are significantly less likely to approach a professor who gives students a rule-laden syllabus.

Wasley, P. (2008b). The syllabus becomes a repository of legalese. *Chronicle of Higher Education, 54*(27), A1–A10.

The author interviews professors on the goals of a syllabus: Is it meant to prevent conflict, or is it meant to be learner centered? She discusses a learner-centered syllabus created collaboratively by a professor who comes to class with a tentative time line of readings and written assignments and his or her students.

Wiggins, G., & McTighe, J. (2005). *Understanding by design.* Alexandria, VA: Association for Supervision and Curriculum Development.

This book shares an excellent overview and step-by-step process for creating a syllabus using backward design, as well as templates and other tools. See the Jay McTighe and Associates website (http://jaymctighe.com/resources/) for extensive online resources for creating syllabi.

Workshop A.2
Strategies for the First and Last Days of Class

By giving students an interesting and inviting introduction, I was able to reduce anxiety about the course and help students view the class as a collaborative learning process. Every field has its own exciting research or striking examples, and it is a good idea to present a few of these up front. The teaching challenge is to find special ideas within your own field. Your class will thank you.

—Kevin L. Bennett (2004)

The first day of class is a terrific opportunity to motivate students, demonstrate why your subject matters, create a greater sense of wonder, and surprise students with how your class might change how they look at the world.

—José Bowen (2012)

Strategies for the First Day of Class

The first day of class sets the tone for the rest of the course. It is an opportunity to engage students and to trigger prior knowledge about course material. The level of participation on the first day of class will send students a strong message about expectations for the rest of the semester. Prepare students for the semester by employing relevant classroom strategies from day one; ask them to participate in a discussion, write a brief passage, give a short oral presentation, or work in groups. These activities will promote community building, which is important to help students begin to feel more connected to the instructor and to the class (Pascarella & Terenzini, 2005). Students will leave a successful first day of class interested in taking the course and in learning the topics presented.

The following are some strategies for creating a learning environment on the first day of class:

- *Predicting class topics based on prior knowledge.* Lyons, McIntosh, and Kysilka (2003) suggest the following exercise:
  - Ask each student to create a list of topics that he or she hopes or predicts will be included in the class.
  - Have students share their ideas with another student and then create categories of ideas based on the discussion. They should give these categories names.
  - Have the pairs join another pair of students and combine ideas. The groups should arrange their categories into a logical sequence on a sheet of chart paper, a laptop, or a tablet to share with the class.

        o Use this information to structure a general course outline. Explain to students that while their ideas will be incorporated into the course, instructors have a responsibility to ensure that the course conforms to university guidelines. Assure students that many of their ideas line up with a rough draft of an agenda that has already been created by the instructor. Before the next class meeting, create the formal syllabus and course agenda to meet the stated description and course objectives, including student input (see Workshop A.1: The Syllabus, p. 61).

- *Writing and sharing basic introductions.* Distribute to each student a half sheet of paper with questions such as, (a) What is your name? (b) What is your hometown? (c) What is your favorite book? (d) What is your favorite film? (e) What is a little known but interesting fact about yourself? Then go around the room and read from these sheets. Even the shyest student is able to read the prepared responses.

Instructional Applications

Weimer (2013) shares some first-day-of-class activities that ask students to think about how they best learn and that stress student responsibilities in creating a positive classroom environment:

Best and Worst Classes

On the first day of class, instructors ask students to recall the best and worst classes they have taken. The students are then asked to go to the board and respond to the prompts "what the teacher did" and "what the students did" in their best and worst classes. When the students read what their classmates have shared, it quickly becomes apparent that student effort is a key ingredient to have a "best class experience" (Weimer, 2013).

First Day Graffiti

This is an adaptation of an activity proposed by Barbara Goza (1993; as cited in Weimer, 2013). Place flip charts with markers or tablets around the classroom. On each chart the instructor writes the beginning of a sentence the students must complete. Some examples are as follows:

> "I have trouble participating in class when . . . "
> "I feel most comfortable contributing to class discussion when . . . "
> "I have had successful learning experiences when . . . "

As students walk around the room and write their answers, they are encouraged to talk about their responses with their peers and their instructor. Once there are comments on each flip chart, the instructor can talk about several of the responses and tell the students what they can expect during the semester.

Syllabus Speed Dating

This first-day-of-class activity was created by Karen Eifler (as cited in Weimer, 2013), a University of Portland education professor. Two rows of chairs face each other so that students can sit across from one another. The instructor asks the students, working in pairs, to discuss two questions. One question is a personal interest question, and the other is about the syllabus. The questions allow the students to get to know each other and discuss important aspects of the course. Once students have had a few minutes to chat about the first two questions, those in one row move down a seat to form new pairs. The instructor then asks a different set of questions.

Online Resources

Cox, K. J. (2005). Group introductions—Get-acquainted team building activity. Retrieved from http://www.docstoc.com/docs/34260610/Group-Introductions-Get-Acquainted-Team-Building

This document, which includes questions for reflection, presents a method for student introductions for group work or small classes.

Fleming, N. (2003). *Establishing rapport: Personal interaction and learning* (IDEA Paper No. 39). Retrieved from Idea Center website: http://www.theideacenter.org/sites/default/files/IDEA_Paper_39.pdf

This paper discusses the relationship between rapport and motivation. It also notes the importance of rapport as a predictor of outcomes.

Iowa State University, Center for Excellence in Learning and Teaching. (2011). Welcoming students on the first day [Video]. Retrieved from http://www.celt.iastate.edu/teaching/video/welcoming.html

This video is part of a series about creating a positive learning environment.

Palmer, M. (n.d.). Not quite 101 ways to learn students' names. Retrieved from University of Virginia Teaching Resource Center website: http://trc.virginia.edu/teaching-tips/not-quite-101-ways-to-learning-students-names/

This resource provides many tips for remembering student names. It includes standard methods, such as flash cards and memorization, and more inventive strategies, such as scavenger hunts.

Strategies for the Last Day of Class

The last day of class can serve as a culminating experience or as a transition to continued learning by the student.
—Endicott College Center for Teaching Excellence

The last day of class can be a transformative and exciting experience for both professors and students. It is a moment when students can reflect on what they have accomplished, how much they have learned, and how their new knowledge will be relevant to their future.

Strategies for inviting reflection and providing closure include the following:

- Ask students to write three of the most important ideas they learned in class. After 10 minutes of writing, invite students to share what they have written. Participating in this discussion helps students develop a better understanding of what they have learned (Lang, 2006).
- On the first day of class, ask students to complete an information sheet about what they hope to learn in class. On the last day of class, return those sheets and asks them to discuss "whether they fulfilled their hopes or learned something new" (Lang, 2006).
- Ask students to write a letter to future students, giving them advice about how to succeed in the class. This can be a good way for students to reflect on how much they have learned during the semester.
- Ask the class as a whole to construct a concept map of the course, demonstrating their understanding of how the course worked. Appoint three students, each with a different color marker, to be the artists and invite the rest of the students to make suggestions. Alternatively, have groups of five to six students create posters using self-sticking posters. (See Workshop 1.1: Concept Maps, p. 9.)
- Ask students to think about how course material might be pertinent to their future. This can help give learning more meaning and can close the course on a positive note.
- Invite students to review the syllabus to reaffirm that learning outcomes have been met and to remind them of the material that has been covered. Ask them what they think they will remember or use the longest. Ask them what will make the greatest and least impact on their learning goals and personal life.
- If you assessed student knowledge in the first few days of class via a pretest, use the pretest again on the last day as a type of posttest. This will help students recognize how much they have learned during the semester.

Appendix B

WORKSHOP ON LECTURES AND MINI-LECTURES

A lecture is much more of a dialogue than many of you probably realize.
—George Wald (1969)

Workshop B.1
Planning and Delivery

For many instructors lectures are part and parcel of their teaching. Hoyt and Perera (2000) reported that 45% of faculty sampled in a study listed lecture as their primary method of teaching. Well-crafted lectures that include active-learning strategies tend to be the most effective (Nilson, 2010). Bligh (2000) and McKeachie and Svinicki (2013) provide several situations in which the lecture is the most effective teaching method, including giving students a personal viewpoint on the reading, updating students on new material not yet available, modeling a problem-solving approach, and clarifying a complex concept in the reading. Note the absence of lecturing on material that duplicates what students have read. Active-learning activities are more beneficial to students' learning than listening to a lecture on material that they were assigned to read (Nilson, 2010).

Planning

First, you will need to establish learning goals. Often the act of creating learning goals brings a course into sharper focus, thus reducing the amount of material to be studied. Although scaling back on the amount of content can be challenging for many college instructors, the result can be that students focus on the primary goals of the course rather than on the superficial.

Rather than using lectures to convey factual information, use them as a means for posing problems and raising issues. Students can be held accountable for finding facts in their reading, leaving instructors free to devote lectures to synthesis and analysis.

Delivery

Opening Strategies

Students tend to best remember information or experiences presented first; they remember second best what is presented at the end of class. Their recall of skills and concepts taught just past the middle of class is weakest. These findings are known respectively as "primacy" and "recency" in the serial position effect (Burns, 1985; Reed, 2006; Terry, 2005). Capitalize on the primacy/recency effect by introducing the most important information at the beginning of class, when retention tends to be best. Following are some opening strategies:

- Begin with a high-level question or quotation from the day's reading that will be further developed in class. Ask students to discuss the question or quotation with a partner, write about it, or respond to it verbally (see Think-Pair-Share, pp. 34 and 46).
- Open with a story, anecdote, question-and-answer session, or demonstration related to the lecture.
- Ask students to spend a few minutes writing about the readings for the day.
- Briefly share the broad goals of the day's class before moving to the specifics. Connect these goals to the previous class material to reinforce their importance.

The Interactive Lecture

For an effective interactive lecture, divide the material into 10–15 minute chunks, or mini-lectures (Medina, 2008). Separate these chunks with active-learning activities. These activities can range from 2 to 15 minutes in length and will serve to reboot the lecture, give students a break, and encourage students to interact with the lecture content, their notes, and each other. Alternating between mini-lectures, discussion, and activities allows students time to assimilate what they've learned. In addition, students know that the pace will change often, so they are more apt to stay engaged in class. Some strategies to keep students engaged during lectures include the following:

- Do not overload students. Students lose sight of the main ideas when too many details are given or when too many ideas are presented and not developed. Engage students more fully with less material. If the material is well developed, students will learn better.
- Help students relate new material to something they already know. Build on their past experience and coursework to help connect new material to old. The human brain is constantly seeking meaning and pattern in facts, memories, and emotions (Davis, 2008). (See Principle 3: Emotion and Relevance Deepen Learning, p. 15.)
- Connect information with values and feelings so that it will be more readily learned. Students should be encouraged to develop passionate stances on issues so that they will retain information more efficiently. (See Principle 3: Emotion and Relevance Deepen Learning, p. 15.)
- Organize material in a logical order, such as cause-effect, chronological, contrast and comparison, problem-solution, pro-con, or importance.

- Most students learn best from a combination of aural, visual, and verbal presentations. Use visuals to increase understanding and impact. (See Principle 4: Multisensory Instruction Deepens Learning, p. 25.)
- For projected text, use a large font in a dark color and leave some lights on in the room to allow students to take notes.
- A good lecture involves a dialogue between the instructor and students, even if the instructor delivers longer prepared remarks before inviting responses. Interactive exercises help students learn and retain more details than does passive listening for extended periods.

Focus on Speaking Skills

To maintain student engagement, it is important to consider these speaking skills:

- Vary speech from loud to soft, quick to slow, excited to calm.
- Pause to get students' attention and to give them time to take notes.
- Enunciate clearly.
- Be expressive with face and hands.
- Move freely away from class notes while lecturing. Walk around in front of the class rather than staying anchored to lecture notes. The more audience members are encouraged to pay attention to movement and change, the less likely they are to lose interest.
- Be encouraging and welcoming.
- Speak from an outline that will allow organization of thoughts in a coherent manner. Do not write out the lecture, as this will lead to reading from notes and a poor delivery; instead, provide general topic headings and a few key details or sentences that should be included.
- Keep text to a minimum in projected slides, such as a PowerPoint presentation, and focus more on images (see Principle 4: Multisensory Instruction Deepens Learning, p. 25).

Closure

A strong conclusion to the class is important as it can solidify learning of new skills and concepts presented that day. Plan to use the last few minutes of class to have students summarize key points and make connections to past and future topics. A short in-class practice test or 1-minute paper can be invaluable to help students review and retain the material discussed in class (Karpicke & Blunt, 2011; Roediger & Karpicke, 2006). (See Principle 6: Formative Assessment or Low-Stakes Evaluation Strengthens Retention, p. 43.)

Annotated Research Studies

Huxham, M. (2005). Learning in lectures: Do "interactive windows" help? *Active Learning in Higher Education, 6*(1), 17–31.

"Interactive windows" are activities embedded in a lecture, such as discussions, problem-solving exercises, and think-pair-share. Huxham examined the use of these short interactive windows in lectures over a 5-year period. Teaching evaluations involving more than 500 responses showed that the "interactive windows" were the most popular aspect of the courses. The classes that were taught interactively showed strong evidence of their positive influence on recall and learning.

Terry, W. (2005). Serial position effects in recall of television commercials. *Journal of General Psychology, 132*(2), 151–163.

College students viewed lists of 15 commercials and were asked to recall the product brand names. When tested, they easily remembered the first commercials (a primacy effect) and the last (a recency effect). Their ability to remember the products from commercials viewed in the middle, however, was significantly lower. In a test administered at the end of the term, recall of the first items persisted, whereas recall of the middle and last items disappeared.

Online Resources

Denman, M. (2005). How to create memorable lectures. *Speaking of Teaching, 14*(1), 1–5. Retrieved from http://www.stanford.edu/dept/CTL/Newsletter/memorable_lectures.pdf

Drummond, T. (1995). A brief summary of the best practices in college teaching. Retrieved from University of North Carolina–Charlotte Center for Teaching and Learning website: http://teaching.uncc.edu/articles-books/best-practice-articles/course-development/best-practices

Hamm, P. H. (2006). *Teaching and persuasive communication: Class presentation skills.* Retrieved from Brown University Harriet W. Sheridan Center for Teaching and Learning website: http://brown.edu/about/administration/sheridan-center/sites/brown.edu.about.administration.sheridan-center/files/uploads/Teaching%20and%20Persuasive%20Communication.pdf

University of California–Berkeley, Center for Teaching and Learning. (n.d.). Large lecture classes: Six ways to make lectures in a large enrollment course more manageable and effective. Retrieved from http://teaching.berkeley.edu/large-lecture-classes

University of Minnesota, Center for Teaching and Learning. (2010). Planning lectures. Retrieved from http://www1.umn.edu/ohr/teachlearn/tutorials/lectures/planning/index.html

Appendix C

WORKSHOP ON CLASSROOM DISCUSSIONS

The exceptional teachers did not just want to get students speaking; they wanted them to think and learn how to engage in an exchange of ideas.

—Ken Bain (2004)

The classroom ought to be a place where things are said seriously— not without pleasure, not without joy—but seriously, and for serious consideration. . . . I see it as a fundamental responsibility of the teacher to show by example the ability to listen to others seriously.

—bell hooks (1994)

Workshop C.1
Classroom Discussions

The purpose of class discussion is to enrich the understanding of a topic or text. Professors can also use discussions to generate interaction following a section of a lecture. In-class discussions engage students with a topic, encourage student participation, and help develop important speaking and listening skills. Brookfield and Preskill (2005) point out that discussion promotes habits of good discourse, helps students learn to synthesize and integrate new information, permits students to test out their ideas against the opinions of others, and allows different perspectives to be heard. Moreover, discussion is a crucial process for students to learn how to construct knowledge through grappling with complex ideas and raising questions. However, these goals are achieved only if the discussion is a success. Brookfield and Preskill (2005, pp. 37–39) suggest that the primary reasons discussions fail are unrealistic expectations, lack of ground rules, perceived unwelcoming classroom environment, unprepared students, and no teacher modeling. This workshop is designed to offer some techniques for inspiring successful class discussions.

Guidelines for Good Discussions

Define *Participation*

- Instructors are encouraged to define what they mean by *participation*. Students need to understand that class discussions are about developing good habits of discourse, that is, both speaking and listening. Extroverted students must understand that part of their role in creating a constructive discussion is to leave room for the shy students to speak, while introverted students must make an effort to contribute. It is essential that students know that they are not having a dialogue with the professor but instead with their peers. They must listen and respond to one another. Motivate students to pay attention by making it explicit that they need to take notes on what their classmates say.

Be Transparent

Students are more willing to participate if they recognize the value of class discussion. When they understand that they are developing skills that will help them in the future, they are more likely to take class discussion seriously.

Give Participation a Value

Make it clear early that participation is expected. Instructors are encouraged to inform students that participation will be a component of their grade.

Get Students Involved

Bain (2004) believes that the longer students sit without entering the discussion the harder it will be for them to participate. Early in the term, it is especially important to devise ways for each student to have something to say. (See the following instructional applications for specific suggestions.) Allowing students time to collect their thoughts is one of the surest ways to get students to engage in the discussion. If instructors give students time to write about a topic before beginning a discussion, students will be more likely to have something useful to offer. Highly structured group work can also foster a safe environment for students to participate in discussions (see Principle 5: Small Groups Engage Students, p. 32). When students have a clear understanding of their role in a conversation, they often feel more comfortable critiquing, questioning, and challenging. Group work has the added benefit of allowing students to practice articulating their ideas with a few peers before sharing them with the entire class. If students are resisting participating in class discussion, it may be wise to invite them to contribute.

Encourage Student Preparation

To participate, students must be prepared for class. Bain (2004) advocates treating readings as sources for solving problems or raising issues. Nilson (2010) suggests having students take notes on readings or write reactions or summaries; then allow students to use their summaries in class. Instructors can also send students study questions and permit them to use their answers during in-class discussion. This both prepares students and gives them confidence to speak.

Choose Relevant Topics

If topics are relevant and important to the students, they are more likely to participate. Bain (2004) suggests that students are more willing to ask questions about something that perplexes, stirs, frustrates, or outrages them. It is also important for instructors to press students for evidence substantiating their ideas. Instructors can encourage students to question and challenge one another and the instructors themselves.

Pose Good Questions

Ross (1860) wrote, "To question well is to teach well." Some approaches to encourage students to think critically through effective questioning include the following:

- Pose questions that require analysis and synthesis. This aids students in formulating their thoughts and constructing solid arguments rather than encouraging simple recall. (See Bloom's taxonomy, p. 45.)
- Consider using a question-based structure, such as the Socratic method, for class discussion (see Stanford University, 2003).
- Create questions by working backward from the course goals. Such questions require instructors to think about the primary "take-away message" of their class and then to create questions that will guide students to grapple with thought-provoking issues (Nilson, 2010).

Model Listening

Students must feel that they are heard, respected, and taken seriously for discussion to work well, and they must see that their professors listen to them and their peers. When students are asked to engage their imaginations and articulate their thoughts, instructors may hear wrong answers. Rather than correcting a wrong response, instructors can ask students questions that help them articulate their thought process and explore new ideas. By asking students to reflect on their own thinking, instructors model important metacognitive skills. (See metacognition, p. 4.)

Wrap Up

Students may find it difficult to know the objective of a discussion class (another reason to make it explicit that in-class discussion is meant to develop their speaking, listening, and critical-thinking skills). To alleviate student anxiety, provide a wrap-up of the day's discussion. Nilson (2010) suggests randomly selecting a student to summarize the major points made in class and then asking others to contribute their opinions. Professors may also want to ask concluding questions about what was learned and what else students should know.

Instructional Applications

Bring Quotes to Class

Ask students to bring a meaningful quote from the reading to class on an index card. Have students read their quotes at the beginning of class to generate discussion. A variation of this activity is to have students anonymously drop their quotes into a box as they enter the class. Then choose a student (perhaps a quiet one) to select a quote to read and have the class discuss the passage.

Generate Questions

Invite students to prepare questions before class and to turn in these questions at the beginning of class. Ask a student to select a question to discuss. Students may also be asked to write one or more questions before class and then lead discussion of their questions. They can also work in small groups and determine a question for the class to answer, and then the groups can lead discussion about their questions.

Recall Concrete Images

This strategy is especially helpful for getting quieter students to talk. Invite each student to recall an important event or image from the text. List these images on the board. Remembering concrete scenes often prompts further recollections. The instructor can then ask follow-up questions, such as, "What themes emerge from this list?"

Shift Points of View

After discussing a text or question from one viewpoint, ask students to consider another perspective. Compare and contrast the strengths and weaknesses, or benefits and disadvantages, of different views.

Take a Poll

Prepare students for the day's topic by polling them before the discussion. This can be done prior to or at the beginning of class using student response instruments (clickers) or Twitter. A poll will provide a picture of where the class stands and allow students to see they are not alone in their opinions. This will make them more comfortable sharing their views.

Generate Truth Statements

To develop critical skills and generate "friendly rivalry" among groups, divide students into groups and instruct each group to choose three statements that are true about a particular issue. Frederick (1981) gives these examples:

"It is true about slavery that . . . "
"We have agreed that it is true about the welfare system that . . . "
"It is true about international politics in the 1950s that . . . "
"We know it to be true about the theory of relativity that . . . "

This strategy generates discussion not only inside the groups as they have to agree what is "true" but also in the class as a whole. It also reveals student assumptions about an issue while demanding that they analyze their own assumptions. (For additional strategies on leading discussions, see Frederick, 1981.)

Lead a Circular Response Discussion

Brookfield and Preskill (2005) suggest a circular response discussion for honing student listening skills. For this exercise students sit in a circle and are given a prompt to discuss. Each speaker has 1 minute to address the prompt, but the speaker must incorporate the comments of the preceding speaker. The speakers do not have to agree with the comments that have already been made, but they do have to use them as a springboard for their own comments. This exercise encourages both respectful listening and respectful disagreement. The rules that Brookfield and Preskill (2005, p. 80) outline are as follows:

- No one interrupts the speaker.
- No one speaks out of turn.
- Each person is allowed 1 minute (or so, to be determined by the size of the class and the goals of the professor).
- Each person strives to show how his or her comments respond to the comments of the previous speaker.

Assign Conversational Roles

Brookfield (2006, pp. 146–147) suggests that to have a fruitful discussion, students can be assigned roles for the discussion. It is important that if instructors use this technique on a regular basis, they must have students alternate roles. Some of the suggested roles are as follows:

- Theme poser: This person posits the problem or issue to be discussed.
- Reflective analyst: This person occasionally summarizes what he or she hears during the conversation.
- Devil's advocate: When there seems to be a consensus, this person offers another view.
- Detective: This person challenges unchecked or unchallenged biases.
- Textual focuser: This person requires that the discussants back up their assertions with text.

Videos

Harvard University, Derek Bok Center for Teaching and Learning. (2007, September 4). Derek Bok Center: The art of discussion leading [YouTube video]. Retrieved from http://www.youtube.com/watch?v=G53os5becKU

Professor Roland Christenson from the Harvard Business School demonstrates and shares tips on how to lead a good discussion.

Otis College of Art and Design. (2009, July 18). Otis teaching tips: Leading classroom discussions [YouTube video]. Retrieved from http://www.youtube.com/watch?v=T_BAN-RJZedU

Heather Joseph-Witham from the Otis College of Art and Design shares ideas and examples for leading class discussions.

Online Resources

For definitions and examples of discussion protocols see the following sources:

Looking at Student Work. (n.d.) Protocols. Retrieved from http://www.lasw.org/protocols.html
McDonald, J. P., Zydney, J. M., Dichter, A., & McDonald, E. C. (2012). Abbreviated protocols. Retrieved from Teachers College Press website: http://www.tcpress.com/pdfs/mcdonaldprot.pdf

BIBLIOGRAPHY

Preface

Persellin, D., & Daniels, M. (2012). *Strengthening undergraduate learning: Six research-based principles for teaching and applications.* Atlanta, GA: Associated Colleges of the South.

Introduction

Ambrose, S. A., Bridges, M. W., DiPietro, M., Lovett, M. C., & Norman, M. K. (2010). *How learning works: Seven research-based principles for smart teaching* (pp. 10–39). San Francisco, CA: Jossey-Bass.

Argyris, C. (2002). Teaching smart people how to learn. *Reflections, 4*(2), 4–15.

Atkinson, R. C., & Shiffrin, R. M. (1968). Human memory: A proposed system and its control processes. In K. W. Spence & J. T. Spence (Eds.), *The psychology of learning and motivation* (Vol. 2, pp. 89–195). New York, NY: Academic Press.

Baddeley, A. D. (1986). *Working memory* (Oxford Psychology Series No. 11). Oxford, UK: Clarendon Press.

Baxter-Magolda, M. (1992). *Knowing and reasoning in college: Gender-related patterns in students' intellectual development.* San Francisco, CA: Jossey-Bass.

Belenky, M. F., Clinchy, B. M., Goldberger, N. R., & Tarule, J. R. (1986). *Women's ways of knowing.* New York, NY: Basic Books.

Bransford, J. D., Brown, A. L., & Cocking, R. R. (Eds.). (2000). *How people learn: Brain, mind, experience, and school.* Washington DC: National Academies Press.

Bransford, J. D., & Schwartz, D. (1999). Rethinking transfer: A simple proposal with multiple implications. *Review of Research in Education, 24,* 61–100.

Braun, A., & Bock, J. (2007). Born to learn: Early learning optimizes brain function. In W. Gruhn & F. Rauscher (Eds.), *Neurosciences and music pedagogy* (pp. 27–51). New York, NY: Nova Science.

Caine, G., Caine, R. N., McClintic, C., & Klimek, K. (2005). *12 brain/mind learning principles in action.* Thousand Oaks, CA: Corwin Press.

Chin, C., & Brown, D. (2000). Learning in science: A comparison of deep and surface approaches. *Journal of Research in Science Teaching, 37*(2), 136.

Deutsch, J. (2004). Memory: Experimental approaches. In R. Gregory (Ed.), *Oxford companion to the mind* (2nd ed., pp. 568–571). New York, NY: Oxford University Press.

Doyle, T., & Zakrajsek, T. (2013). *The new science of learning: How to learn in harmony with your brain*. Sterling, VA: Stylus.

Kember, D., Ho, A., & Hong, C. (2008). The importance of establishing relevance in motivating student learning. *Active Learning in Higher Education, 9*(3), 249–263.

King, P. M., & Kitchener, K. S. (2004). Reflective judgment: Theory and research on the development of epistemic assumptions through adulthood. *Educational Psychologist, 39*(1), 5–18.

Kloss, R. J. (1994). A nudge is best: Helping students through the Perry scheme of intellectual development. *College Teaching, 42*(4), 151–158.

McLeod, S. A. (2007). Multi store model of memory—Atkinson and Shiffrin, 1968. Retrieved from Simply Psychology website: http://www.simplypsychology.org/multi-store.html

Medina, J. (2008). *Brain rules* (pp. 95–119). Seattle, WA: Pear Press.

Moore, W. S. (1989). The learning environment preferences: Exploring the construct validity of an objective measure of the Perry scheme of intellectual development. *Journal of College Student Development, 30*, 504–514.

National Research Council. (2001). *Knowing what students know: The science and design of educational assessment*. Washington DC: National Academies Press.

Nilson, L. B. (2013). *Creating self-regulated learners: Strategies to strengthen students' self-awareness and learning skills*. Sterling, VA: Stylus.

Overstreet, K. (2007). PowerPoint activities. Retrieved from http://teach.fcps.net/trt10/PowerPoint.htm

Perry, W. G. (1970). *Forms of ethical and intellectual development in the college years: A scheme*. San Francisco, CA: Jossey-Bass.

Perry Network. (n.d.). Retrieved from http://www.perrynetwork.org/

Skillen, P. (n.d.). Expert learners. Retrieved from Construction Zone website: http://theconstructionzone.wordpress.com/the-construction-zone/expert-learners/

Sousa, D. (2006). *How the brain learns*. Thousand Oaks, CA: Corwin Press.

Squire, L. (2004). Memory systems of the brain: A brief history and current perspective. *Neurobiology of Learning and Memory, 82*(3), 171–177.

Squire, L., Berg, D., Bloom, F., du Lac, S., & Ghosh, A. (2008). *Fundamental neuroscience* (3rd ed.). Burlington, MA: Academic Press.

Sviniki, M. (2004). *Learning and motivation in the postsecondary classroom*. Bolton, MA: Anker.

Vanderbilt University, Center for Teaching. (n.d.). How people learn. Retrieved from http://cft.vanderbilt.edu/teaching-guides/pedagogical/how-people-learn/

Wirth, K., & Perkins, D. (2007). Learning to learn. Retrieved from http://cgiss.boisestate.edu/~billc/Teaching/Items/learningtolearn.pdf

Zull, J. E. (2002). *The art of changing the brain: Enriching the practice of teaching by exploring the biology of learning* (pp. 13–29). Sterling, VA: Stylus.

Chapter 1

Principle 1

Alter, A., Oppenheimer, D., Epley, N., & Eyre, R. (2007). Overcoming intuition: Metacognitive difficulty activates analytic reasoning. *Journal of Experimental Psychology: General, 136*(4), 569–576.

Bain, R., & Zimmerman, J. (2009). Understanding great teaching. *Peer Review, 11*(2). Retrieved from http://www.aacu.org/peerreview/pr-sp09/pr-sp09_bain-zimmerman.cfm

Bjork, E. L., & Bjork, R. A. (2011). Making things hard on yourself, but in a good way: Creating desirable difficulties to enhance learning. In M. A. Gernsbacher, R. W. Pew, L. M. Hough, & J. R. Pomerantz (Eds.), *Psychology and the real world: Essays illustrating fundamental contributions to society* (pp. 56–64). New York, NY: Worth Publishers.

Bjork, R. A. (1994). Memory and metamemory considerations in the training of human beings. In J. Metcalfe & A. Shimamura (Eds.), *Metacognition: Knowing about knowing* (pp. 185–205). Cambridge, MA: MIT Press.

Bjork, R. A. (2013). Applying cognitive psychology to enhance educational practice. Retrieved from University of California–Los Angeles Bjork Learning and Forgetting Lab website: http://bjorklab.psych.ucla.edu/research.html

Bye, J. (2011, May 5). Desirable difficulties in the classroom [web log post]. *Psychology Today*. Retrieved from http://www.psychologytoday.com/blog/all-about-addiction/201105/desirable-difficulties-in-the-classroom

Cepeda, N. J., Pashler, H., Vul, E., Wixted, J. T., & Rohrer, D. (2006). Distributed practice in verbal recall tasks: A review and quantitative synthesis. *Psychological Bulletin, 132*, 354–380.

Dempster, F., & Farris, R. (1990). The spacing effect: Research and practice. *Journal of Research and Development in Education, 23*(2), 97–101.

Didau, D. (2013, June 10). Deliberately difficult—Why it's better to make learning harder [web log post]. *Learning Spy*. Retrieved from http://www.learningspy.co.uk/featured/deliberately-difficult-focussing-on-learning-rather-than-progress/

Diemand-Yauman, C., Oppenheimer, D., & Vaughan, E. (2011). Fortune favors the Bold (and the Italicized): Effects of disfluency on educational outcomes. *Cognition, 118*(1), 111–115. doi:10.1016/j.cognition.2010.09.012

Hermida, J. (n.d.). Deep learning. Retrieved from http://www.julianhermida.com/algoma/law1scotldeeplearning.htm

Karpicke, J., & Blunt, J. (2011). Retrieval practice produces more learning than elaborative studying with concept mapping. *Science, 331*(6018), 772–775. doi:10.1126/science.1199327

Linn, M. C., & Bjork, R. A. (2006). The science of learning and the learning of science: Introducing desirable difficulties. *Observer, 19*(3). Retrieved from http://www.psychologicalscience.org/index.php/publications/observer/2006/march-06/the-science-of-learning-and-the-learning-of-science.html

McDaniel, M., & Butler, A. C. (2010). A contextual framework for understanding when difficulties are desirable. In A. S. Benjamin (Ed.), *Successful remembering and successful forgetting: Essays in honor of Robert A. Bjork* (pp. 175–199). New York, NY: Psychology Press.

McDaniel, M., Hines, R., Waddill, P., & Einstein, G. (1994). What makes folk tales unique: Content familiarity, causal structure, scripts, or superstructures? *Journal of Experimental Psychology: Learning, Memory, and Cognition, 20*(1), 169–184.

McNamara, D. S., Kintsch, E., Songer, N. B., & Kintsch, W. (1996). Are good texts always better? Interactions of text coherence, background knowledge, and levels of understanding in learning from text. *Cognition and Instruction, 14*(1), 1–43. doi:10.1207/s1532690xci1401_1

Roediger, H., & Karpicke, J. (2006). Test-enhanced learning taking memory tests improves long-term retention. *Psychological Science, 17*(3), 249–255.

Rohrer, D., & Taylor, K. (2007). The shuffling of mathematics practice problems improves learning. *Instructional Science, 35*, 481–498.

Yue, C. L., Castel, A. D., & Bjork, R. A. (2013). When disfluency is—and is not—a desirable difficulty: The influence of typeface clarity on metacognitive judgments and memory. *Memory and Cognition, 41*(2), 229–241.

Workshop 1.1

Baume, D., & Baume, C. (2008). *Powerful ideas in teaching and learning*. Wheatley, UK: Oxford Brookes University.

Beissner, K. L. (1991). Use of *concept mapping* to improve problem solving. *Journal of Physical Therapy, 6*(1), 22–27.

Budd, J. W. (2004). Mind maps as classroom exercises. *Journal of Economic Education, 35*(1), 35–46.

Buzan, T. (1995). *The mind map book* (2nd ed.). London, UK: BBC Books.

Clark, C. (2011, May 10). Best tools and practices for concept mapping [web log post]. *NspireD²*. Retrieved from http://ltlatnd.wordpress.com/2011/05/10/best-tools-and-practices-for-concept-mapping/

Daly, B. (2004). Using concept maps with adult students in higher education. In A. J. Cañas, J. D. Novak, & F. M. González (Eds.), *Concept maps: Theory, methodology, technology: Proceedings of the First International Conference on Concept Mapping* (Vol. 1, pp. 183–190). Retrieved from http://cmc.ihmc.us/cmc2004 Proceedings/cmc2004%20-%20Vol%201.pdf

Eppler, M. (2006). A comparison between concept maps, mind maps, conceptual diagrams, and visual metaphors as complementary tools for knowledge construction and sharing. *Information and Visualization, 5*, 202–210.

Horton, P. B., McConney, A., Gallo, M., Woods, A., Senn, G., & Hamelin, D. (1993). An investigation of the effectiveness of concept mapping as an instructional tool. *Science Education, 77*(1), 95–111.

Llewellyn, D. (2007). Making the most of the concept maps. *Science Scope, 30*(5), 74–77.

Morse, D., & Jutras, F. (2008). Implementing concept-based learning in a large undergraduate classroom. *Life Sciences Education, 7*(2), 243–253. doi:10.1187/cbe.07-09-0071

Nilson, L. B. (2010). *Teaching at its best: A research-based resource for college instructors* (3rd ed., pp. 243–245). San Francisco, CA: Jossey-Bass.

Novak, J., & Canas, A. (2008). *The theory underlying concept maps and how to construct and use them* (Technical Report IHMC CmapTools 2006-01 Rev 01-2008). Retrieved from Institute for Human and Machine Cognition website: http://cmap.ihmc.us/publications/researchpapers/theorycmaps/theoryunderlying conceptmaps.htm

Zelik, M., Schau, C., Mattern, N., Hall, S., Teague, K., & Bisard, W. (1997). Conceptual astronomy: A novel model for teaching postsecondary science courses. *American Journal of Physics, 6*(10), 987–996. doi:10.1119/1.18702

Principle 2

Bahrick, H. P. (1979). Maintenance of knowledge: Questions about memory we forgot to ask. *Journal of Experimental Psychology: General, 108*(3), 296–308.

Cepeda, N. J., Pashler, H., Vul, E., Wixted, J. T., & Rohrer, D. (2006). Distributed practice in verbal recall tasks: A review and quantitative synthesis. *Psychological Bulletin, 132*, 354–380.

Cull, W. L. (2000). Untangling the benefits of multiple study opportunities and repeated testing for cured recall. *Applied Cognitive Psychology, 14*, 215–223.

Delaney, P. F., Verkoeijen, P. J., & Spirgel, A. (2010). Spacing and testing effects: A deeply critical, lengthy, and at times discursive review of the literature. *Psychology of Learning and Motivation: Advances in Research and Theory, 53*, 63–147.

Dunlosky, J., Rawson, K., Marsh, E., Nathan, M., & Willingham, D. (2013). Improving students' learning with effective learning techniques: Promising directions from cognitive and educational psychology. *Psychological Science in the Public Interest, 14*(1), 4–58. doi:10.1177/1529100612453266

Karpicke, J., & Roediger, H. (2008). The critical importance of retrieval for learning. *Science, 319*(5865), 966. doi:10.1126/science.1152408

Kornell, N. (2009). Optimizing learning using flashcards: Spacing is more effective than cramming. *Applied Cognitive Psychology, 23*, 1297–1317.

Medina, J. (2008). *Brain rules* (pp. 95–119). Seattle, WA: Pear Press.

Meltzoff, A., Kuhl, P., Movellan, J., & Sejnowski, S. (2009). Foundations for a new science of learning. *Science, 325*(5938), 284–288.

Reiser, R. A., & Dempsey, J. V. (2007). *Trends and issues in instructional design* (2nd ed.). Upper Saddle River, NJ: Pearson Education.

Sousa, D. (2006). *How the brain learns.* Thousand Oaks, CA: Corwin Press.

Squire, L. (2004). Memory systems of the brain: A brief history and current perspective. *Neurobiology of Learning and Memory, 82*(3), 171–177.

Zull, J. E. (2002). *The art of changing the brain: Enriching the practice of teaching by exploring the biology of learning* (p. 129). Sterling, VA: Stylus.

Principle 3

Ainley, M. (2006). Connecting with learning: Motivation, affect and cognition in interest processes. *Educational Psychological Review, 18,* 391–405.

Ambrose, S. A., Bridges, M. W., DiPietro, M., Lovett, M. C., & Norman, M. K. (2010). *How learning works: Seven research-based principles for smart teaching* (pp. 153–187). San Francisco, CA: Jossey-Bass.

Braun, A., & Bock, J. (2007). Born to learn: Early learning optimizes brain function. In W. Gruhn & F. Rauscher (Eds.), *Neurosciences and music pedagogy* (pp. 27–51). New York, NY: Nova Science.

Caine, G., Caine, R. N., McClintic, C., & Klimek, K. (2005). *12 brain/mind learning principles in action.* Thousand Oaks, CA: Corwin Press.

Dolan, R. J. (2002). Emotion, cognition, and behavior. *Science, 298*(5596), 1191–1194. doi:10.1126/science.1076358

Hodges, D. (2010). Can neuroscience help us do a better job of teaching music? *General Music Today, 23*(3), 3–12.

Kember, D., Ho, A., & Hong, C. (2008). The importance of establishing relevance in motivating student learning. *Active Learning in Higher Education, 9*(3), 249–263.

Kenny, N. (2010, April 30). Relevance: The secret to motivating student learning [web log post]. *Natasha Kenny's Blog.* Retrieved from http://natashakenny .wordpress.com/2010/04/30/relevance-the-secret-to-motivating-student-learning/

Lattuca, L., & Stark, J. (2009). *Shaping the college curriculum: Academic plans in context.* San Francisco, CA: Jossey-Bass.

Lawson, C. (2012). The connections between emotions and learning. Retrieved from Center for Development and Learning website: http://www.cdl.org/resource-library/articles/connect_emotions.php

Medina, J. (2008). *Brain rules* (pp. 79–82, 215–221). Seattle, WA: Pear Press.

Nilson, L. B. (2010). *Teaching at its best: A research-based resource for college instructors* (3rd ed., pp. 243–245). San Francisco, CA: Jossey-Bass.

Nilson, L. B. (2011). *The mind has a mind of its own: Teaching and learning that's in sync with the mind* [webinar]. Retrieved from Emphasis on Excellence website: http:// www.meggin.com/classes/previous-classes/the-mind-has-a-mind-of-its-own/

Pekrun, R. (1992). The impact of emotions on learning and achievement: Towards a theory of cognitive/motivational mediators. *Applied Psychology, 41*(4), 359–376.

Pekrun, R., Goetz, T., Titz, W., & Perry, R. (2002). Academic emotions in students' self-regulated learning and achievement: A program of qualitative and quantitative research. *Educational Psychologist, 37*(2), 91–106.

Rogan, M. T., Stäubli, U. V., & LeDoux, J. E. (1997). Fear conditioning induces long-term potentiation in the amygdala. *Nature, 390,* 604–607.

Shultz, P., & Pekrun, R. (Eds.). (2007). *Emotion in education.* Burlington, MA: Academic Press.

Sylwester, R. (1994). How emotions affect learning. *Educational Leadership, 52,* 60–65.

Turk-Browne, N. B., Yi, D. J., & Chun, M. M. (2006). Linking implicit and explicit memory: Common encoding factors and shared representations. *Neuron, 49,* 917–927.

Vail, P. L. (2010). The role of emotions in learning. Retrieved from Great Schools website: http://www.greatschools.org/parenting/teaching-values/the-role-of-emo-tions-in-learning.gs?content=751&page=2

Wieman, C. (2007, September-October). Why not try a scientific approach to science education? *Change,* 9–15. Retrieved from http://www.changemag.org/Archives/Back%20Issues/September-October%202007/full-scientific-approach.html

Willis, J. (2006). *Research-based strategies to ignite student learning: Insights from a neurologist and a classroom teacher.* Alexandria, VA: Association for Supervision and Curriculum.

Zull, J. E. (2002). *The art of changing the brain: Enriching the practice of teaching by exploring the biology of learning* (pp. 69–87). Sterling, VA: Stylus.

Workshop 3.1

Boyer, E. (1996). The scholarship of engagement. *Bulletin of the American Academy of Arts and Sciences, 1*(1), 18–33.

Bringle, R., Philips, M., & Hudson, M. (2004). *The measure of service learning: Research scales to assess student experiences.* Washington DC: American Psychological Association.

Campus Compact. (2003). *Introduction to service learning toolkit: Readings and resources for faculty.* Boston, MA: Author.

Correia, M., & Bleicher, R. (2008). Making connections to teach reflection. *Michigan Journal of Community Service Learning, 14*(12), 41–49.

Felten, P., Gilchrist, L. Z., & Darby, A. (2006). Emotion and learning: Feeling our way toward a new theory of reflection in service-learning. *Michigan Journal of Community Service Learning, 12*(2), 38–46.

Hatcher, J. A., Bringle, R. G., & Muthiah, R. (2004). Designing effective reflection: What matters to service-learning? *Michigan Journal of Community Service Learning, 11*(1), 38–46.

Howard, K. (2010–2011). *Community based learning at Centre College: Faculty handbook.* Retrieved from Centre College Center for Teaching and Learning website: http://ctl.centre.edu/assets/cblhandbook.pdf

Jacoby, B. (Ed.). (1996). *Service-learning in higher education.* San Francisco, CA: Jossey-Bass.

Meader, L. (2011). Real money, real lessons. *Colby Magazine, 100*(2). Retrieved from http://www.colby.edu/colby.mag/issues/58/article/1266/real-money-real-lessons/

Chapter 2

Bonwell, C. C., & Eison, J. A. (1991). *Active learning: Creating excitement in the classroom* (ASHE-ERIC Higher Education Report No. 1). Washington DC: George Washington University, School of Education and Human Development.

Brewer, E. W., & Burgess, D. N. (2005). Professor's role in motivating students to attend class. *Journal of Industrial Teacher Education, 42*(23), 23–47.

Codde, J. R. (2006). Applying the seven principles for good practice in undergraduate education. Retrieved from https://www.msu.edu/user/coddejos/seven.htm

Doyle, T. (2008). *Helping students learn in a learner centered environment: A guide to teaching in higher education.* Sterling, VA: Stylus.

Hake, R. (1998). Interactive-engagement vs. traditional methods: A six-thousand-student survey of mechanics test data for introductory physics courses. *American Journal of Physics, 66*(1), 64–74. doi:10.1119/1.18809

Hodara, M. (2011). *Reforming mathematics classroom pedagogy: Evidence-based findings and recommendations for the developmental math classroom* (Working Paper No. 27). New York, NY: Community College Research Center.

Jones-Wilson, T. (2005). Teaching problem-solving skills without sacrificing course content: Marrying traditional lecture and active learning in an organic chemistry class. *Journal of College Science Teaching, 35*(1), 42–46.

Kuh, G. D., Cruce, T. M., Shoup, R., Kinzie, J., & Gonyea, R. M. (2008). Unmasking the effects of student engagement on first-year college grades and persistence. *Journal of Higher Education, 79*, 540–563.

Millis, B. (2010). *Promoting deep learning* (IDEA Paper No. 47). Retrieved from Idea Center website: http://www.theideacenter.org/sites/default/files/IDEA_Paper_47.pdf

Nilson, L. B. (2010). *Teaching at its best: A research-based resource for college instructors* (3rd ed., p. 7). San Francisco, CA: Jossey-Bass.

Pascarella, E. T., & Terenzini, P. T. (2005). *How college affects students: Vol. 2. A third decade of research.* San Francisco, CA: Jossey-Bass.

Prince, M. (2004). Does active learning work? A review of the research. *Journal of Engineering Education, 93*(3), 223–231.

Wood, W. B., & Gentile, J. M. (2003). Teaching in a research context. *Science, 302*(5650), 1510. doi:10.1126/science.1091803

Zull, J. E. (2002). *The art of changing the brain: Enriching the practice of teaching by exploring the biology of learning* (pp. 135–152). Sterling, VA: Stylus.

Principle 4

Delahoussaye, M. (2002). The perfect learner: An expert debate on learning styles. *Training, 39*(5), 28–36.

Fadel, C. (2008). *Multimodal learning through media: What the research says.* Retrieved from Cisco Systems website: http://www.cisco.com/web/strategy/docs/education/Multimodal-Learning-Through-Media.pdf

Gazzaniga, M. (2008). *Learning, arts, and the brain.* Retrieved from Dana Foundation website: http://www.dana.org/uploadedfiles/news_and_publications/special_publications/learning,%20arts%20and%20the%20brain_artsandcognition_compl.pdf

Ginns, P. (2005). Meta-analysis of the modality effect. *Learning and Instruction, 15*, 313–331.

Jones, J. (2009, November 2). Challenging the presentation paradigm (in 6 minutes, 40 seconds): Pecha kucha [web log post]. *ProfHacker.* Retrieved from http://

chronicle.com/blogs/profhacker/challenging-the-presentation-paradigm-in-6-minutes-40-seconds-pecha-kucha/22807

Jones-Wilson, T. (2005). Teaching problem-solving skills without sacrificing course content: Marrying traditional lecture and active learning in an organic chemistry class. *Journal of College Science Teaching, 35*(1), 42–46.

Jung, F. (n.d.). Guide to making a PechaKucha presentation: Overview. Retrieved from http://avoision.com/pechakucha

Kalyuga, S. (2000). When using sound with a text or picture is not beneficial for learning. *Australian Journal of Educational Technology, 16*(2), 161–172.

Kress, G., Jewitt, C., Ogborn, J., & Charalampos, T. (2006). *Multimodal teaching and learning: The rhetorics of the science classroom.* London, UK: Continuum.

Kress, G., & Van Leeuwen, T. (2006). *Reading images: The grammar of visual design.* New York, NY: Routledge.

Mayer, R. E. (2005). Cognitive theory of multimedia learning. In R. E. Mayer (Ed.), *Cambridge handbook of multimedia learning* (pp. 31–48). New York, NY: Cambridge University Press.

Mayer, R. E., & Gallini, J. K. (1990). When is a picture worth a thousand words? *Journal of Educational Psychology, 82*, 715–726.

McKeachie, W. J., & Svinicki, M. D. (2013). *McKeachie's teaching tips:* Strategies, *research and theory for college and university teachers* (14th ed.). Belmont, CA: Wadsworth.

Medina, J. (2008). *Brain rules* (pp. 197–219). Seattle, WA: Pear Press.

National Council of Teachers of English. (2004). NCTE beliefs about the teaching of writing. Retrieved from http://www.readwritethink.org/classroom-resources/lesson-plans/designing-effective-poster-presentations-1076.html

Nilson, L. B. (2010). *Teaching at its best: A research-based resource for college instructors* (3rd ed., pp. 113–125). San Francisco, CA: Jossey-Bass.

Pashler, H., McDaniel, M., Rohrer, D., & Bjork, R. (2008). Learning styles: Concepts and evidence. *Psychological Science in the Public Interest, 9*(3), 105–119. doi:10.1111/j.1539-6053.2009.01038.x

Pieters, R., & Wedel, M. (2004). Attention capture and transfer in advertising: Brand, pictorial, and text-size effects. *Journal of Marketing, 68*(2), 36–50.

Pink, D. (2007). Pecha kucha: Get to the PowerPoint in 20 slides then sit the hell down. *Wired, 15*(9). Retrieved from http://www.wired.com/techbiz/media/magazine/15-09/st_pechakucha

Stenberg, G. (2006). Conceptual and perceptual factors in the picture superiority effect. *European Journal of Cognitive Psychology, 18*(6), 813–847.

Svinicki, M. (2004). *Learning and motivation in the postsecondary classroom.* Bolton, MA: Anker.

Tindall-Ford, S., Chandler, P., & Sweller, J. (1997). When two sensory modes are better than one. *Journal of Experimental Psychology: Applied, 3*(4), 257–287. doi:10.1037/1076-898X.3.4.257

Vekiri, I. (2002). What is the value of graphical displays in learning? *Educational Psychology Review, 14*(3), 261–312.

Workshop 4.1

Aune, S. P. (2008, February 21). 12 screencasting tools for creating video tutorials. Retrieved from Mashable: http://mashable.com/2008/02/21/screencasting-video-tutorials/

Bergmann, J., & Sams, A. (2012). *Flip your classroom: Reach every student in every class every day.* Washington DC: International Society for Technology in Education.

Bodie, G., Powers, W., & Fitch-Hauser, M. (2006, August). Chunking, priming and active learning: Toward an innovative and blended approach to teaching communication-related skills. *Interactive Learning Environments, 14*(2), 119–135.

EDUCAUSE. (2013). 7 things you should know about flipped classrooms. Retrieved from http://www.educause.edu/library/resources/7-things-you-should-know-about-flipped-classrooms

Finkel, E. (2012). Flipping the script in K12. Retrieved from District Administration website: www.districtadministration.com/article/flipping-script-k12

Flipped Learning Network. (2012). Improve student learning and teacher satisfaction with one flip of the classroom. Retrieved from http://flippedlearning1.files.wordpress.com/2012/07/classroomwindowinfographic7-12.pdf

Hamden, N., McKnight, P., McKnight, K., & Arfstrom, K. (2013). *A review of flipped learning.* Retrieved from Flipped Learning Network website: http://www.flippedlearning.org/cms/lib07/VA01923112/Centricity/Domain/41/LitReview_FlippedLearning.pdf

Musallam, R. (2011, October 26). Should you flip your classroom? [web log post]. *Edutopia.* Retrieved from http://www.edutopia.org/blog/flipped-classroom-ramsey-musallam

Nagel, D. (2013, June 18). Report: The 4 pillars of the flipped classroom. *The Journal.* Retrieved from http://thejournal.com/articles/2013/06/18/report-the-4-pillars-of-the-flipped-classroom.aspx?=THENU

Pacansky-Brock, M. (2012). *Best practices for teaching with emerging technology.* New York, NY: Routledge.

Talbert, R. (2013, April 4). Data on whether and how students watch screencasts [web log post]. *Casting Out Nines.* Retrieved from http://chronicle.com/blognetwork/castingoutnines/2013/04/04/data-on-whether-and-how-students-watch-screencasts/?cid=wc&utm_source=wc&utm_medium=en

TED. (2011, March). Salman Khan: Let's use video to reinvent education [TED video]. Retrieved from http://www.ted.com/talks/salman_khan_let_s_use_video_to_reinvent_education.html

University of Texas–Austin, Center for Teaching and Learning. (2013). "Flipping" a class. Retrieved from http://ctl.utexas.edu/teaching/flipping_a_class

Principle 5

Angelo, T., & Cross, P. (1993). *Classroom assessment techniques: A handbook for faculty* (2nd ed.). San Francisco, CA: Jossey-Bass.

Barkley, E. F., Cross, K. P., & Major, C. H. (2004). *Collaborative learning techniques: A handbook for college faculty.* San Francisco, CA: Jossey-Bass.

Bransford, J. D., Brown, A. L., & Cocking, R. R. (Eds.). (2000). *How people learn: Brain, mind, experience, and school.* Washington DC: National Academies Press.

Centre for the Study of Higher Education. (2002). Assessing group work. Retrieved from http://www.cshe.unimelb.edu.au/assessinglearning/03/group.html

Chapman, K., Meuter, M., Toy, D., & Wright, L. (2006). Can't we pick our own groups? The influence of group dynamics and outcomes. *Journal of Management Education, 30,* 557.

DeHaan, R. L. (2005). The impending revolution in undergraduate science education. *Journal of Science Education and Technology, 14*(2), 253–269.

Farrell, J. J., Moog, R. S., & Spencer, J. N. (1999). A guided inquiry general chemistry course. *Journal of Chemical Education, 76*(4), 570–574. doi:10.1021/ed076p570

Felton, P. (2008). Resource review: Visual literacy. *Change, 40*(6), 60–63.

George Mason University, Writing Across the Curriculum. (n.d.). *Peer response groups.* Retrieved from http://wac.gmu.edu/supporting/peer_response.php

Heller, P., & Hollabaugh, M. (1992). Teaching problem solving through cooperative grouping. Part 2: Designing problems and structuring groups. *American Journal of Physics, 60*(7), 637–644.

Hilton, S., & Phillips, F. (2010). Instructor-assigned and student-selected groups: A view from the inside. *Issues in Accounting Education, 25*(1), 15–33.

Jassawalla, A. R., Malshe, A., & Sashittal, H. (2008). Student perceptions of social loafing in undergraduate business classroom teams. *Decision Sciences Journal of Innovative Education, 6*(2), 403–426.

Johnson, D. W., Johnson, R. T., & Smith, K. A. (1991). *Active learning: Cooperation in the college classroom* (pp. 89–100). Edina, MN: Interaction Book.

Johnson, D. W., Johnson, R. T., & Smith, K. A. (1998). Cooperative learning returns to college: What evidence is there that it works? *Change, 20*(4), 26–35.

Kalman, C., Rohar, S., & Wells, D. (2004). Enhancing conceptual change using argumentative essays. *American Journal of Physics, 72*(5), 715–717. doi:10.1119/1.1645285

Levine, A., & Dean, D. R. (2012). *Generation on a tightrope: A portrait of today's college students.* San Francisco, CA: Jossey-Bass.

Lord, T. R. (2001). 101 reasons for using cooperative learning in biology teaching. *American Biology Teacher, 6*(1), 30–38.

Michaelson, L., Knight, A. B., & Fink, L. D. (Eds.). (2002). *Team-based learning: A transformative use of small groups.* Westport, CT: Praeger.

Millis, B. (2002). *Enhancing learning—and more!—through cooperative learning* (IDEA Paper No. 38). Retrieved from Idea Center website: http://www.theidea-center.org/sites/default/files/IDEA_Paper_38.pdf

Millis, B. (2010). *Promoting deep learning* (IDEA Paper No. 47). Retrieved from Idea Center website: http://www.theideacenter.org/sites/default/files/IDEA_Paper_47.pdf

Millis, B. (Ed.). (2010). *Cooperative learning in higher education across the disciplines, across the academy.* Sterling, VA: Stylus.

Millis, B. (2012). *Active learning strategies in face-to-face courses* (IDEA Paper No. 53). Retrieved from Idea Center website: http://www.theideacenter.org/sites/default/files/paperidea_53.pdf

Nilson, L. B. (2002–2003). Helping students help each other: Making peer feedback more valuable. *Essays in Teaching Excellence, 14*(8), 1–2. Retrieved from http://podnetwork.org/content/uploads/V14-N5-Nilson.pdf

Nilson, L. B. (2010). *Teaching at its best: A research-based resource for college instructors* (3rd ed., pp. 155–165). San Francisco, CA: Jossey-Bass.

Plank, K. (Ed.). (2011). *Team teaching: Across the disciplines, across the academy.* Sterling, VA: Stylus.

Plank, K. (2013). *Team teaching* (IDEA Paper No. 55). Retrieved from Idea Center website: http://theideacenter.org/sites/default/files/paperidea55.pdf

Pratt, S. (2003). Cooperative learning strategies. *Science Teacher, 4,* 25–29.

Prince, M. (2004). Does active learning work? A review of the research. *Journal of Engineering Education, 93*(3), 223–231.

Sargent, E. (n.d.). Connecting reading and writing: Inkshedding-to-learn. Retrieved from http://www.mhhe.com/socscience/english/tc/pt/sarg/mginkshd_final.html

Slavin, R. (1991). Synthesis of research on cooperative learning. *Educational Leadership, 48*(5), 71–82. Retrieved from http://www.ascd.org/ASCD/pdf/journals/ed_lead/el_199102_slavin.pdf

Sweet, M. (2012). *Team-based learning in the social sciences and humanities: Group work that works to generate critical thinking and engagement.* Sterling, VA: Stylus.

Weimer, M. (2010). Student-formed or instructor-assigned groups? *Teaching Professor, 24*(4), 2–4.

Weimer, M. (2011, June 10). Group work: Are student-selected groups more effective? Retrieved from Faculty Focus website: http://www.facultyfocus.com/articles/teaching-and-learning/group-work-are-student-selected-groups-more-effective/#sthash.ff5mkxah.dpuf

Weimer, M. (2013). *Learner-centered teaching: Five key changes to teaching* (2nd ed.). San Francisco, CA: Jossey-Bass.

Wenzel, T. (2000). Cooperative student activities as learning devices. *Analytical Chemistry, 72,* 293A–296A.

Williamson, V. M., & Rowe, M. W. (2002). Group problem-solving versus lecture in college-level quantitative analysis: The good, the bad, and the ugly. *Journal of Chemical Education, 79*(9), 1131–1134.

Workshop 5.1

Barron, B., Schwartz, D., Vyer, N., Moore, A., Petrosino, A., Zech, L., & Bransford, J. (1998). Doing with understanding: Lessons from research on problem- and project-based learning. *Journal of the Learning Sciences, 7*(3/4), 271–311.

Bessant, S., Bailey, P., Robinson, Z., Tomkinson, C., Tomkinson, R., Ormerod, R., & Boast, R. (2013). *Problem-based learning: Case study of sustainability education: A toolkit for university educators.* Retrieved from http://www.heacademy.ac.uk/assets/documents/ntfs/Problem_Based_Learning_Toolkit.pdf

Dewey, J. (1906). *The child and the curriculum.* Chicago, IL: University of Chicago Press.

Duch, B. J., Groh, S., & Allen, D. E. (2001). *The power of problem-based learning: A practical "how to" for teaching undergraduate courses in any discipline.* Sterling, VA: Stylus.

Eberlein, T., Kampmeier, J., Minderhout, V., Moog, R., Platt, T., Varma-Nelson, P., & White, H. (2008). Pedagogies of engagement in science: A comparison of PBL, POGIL, and PLTL. *Biochemistry and Molecular Biology Education, 36*(4), 262–273.

Hanson, D. (2006). *Instructor's guide to process-oriented guided-inquiry learning.* Lisle, IL: Pacific Crest. Retrieved from http://pogil.org/uploads/media_items/pogil-instructor-s-guide-1.original.pdf

Hmelo-Silver, C. E. (2004). Problem-based learning: What and how do students learn? *Educational Psychology Review, 16*(3), 235–266. doi:10.1023/B:EDPR.0000034022.16470.f3

Hung, W. (2011). Theory to reality: A few issues in implementing problem-based learning. *Educational Technology Research and Development, 59*(4), 529–552. doi:10.1007/s11423-011-9198-1

Illinois Mathematics and Science Academy, PBL Network. (2013) Retrieved from http://pbln.imsa.edu/

Kuh, G. D., Cruce, T. M., & Shoup, R. (2008). Unmasking the effects of student engagement on first-year college grades and persistence. *Journal of Higher Education, 79,* 540–563.

Kuh, G. D., Kinzie, J., Schuh, J. H., & Whitt, E. J. (2005). *Student success in college: Creating conditions that matter.* San Francisco, CA: Jossey-Bass.

Major, C. H., & Palmer, B. (2001). Assessing the effectiveness of problem-based learning in higher education: Lessons from the literature. *Academic Exchange Quarterly, 5*(1), 4–9.

Rangachari, P. K. (2002). Prolegomena to problem writing. In *Writing problems: A personal casebook.* Retrieved from http://fhs.mcmaster.ca/pbls/writing/intro.htm

Schmidt, H., Rotgans, J., & Yew, E. (2011). The process of problem-based learning: What works and why. *Medical Education, 45*(8), 792–806. doi:10.1111/j.1365-2923.2011.04035.x

Stanford University. (n.d.). *Problem-based learning: Examples of PBL problems.* Retrieved from http://ldt.stanford.edu/~jeepark/jeepark+portfolio/PBL/example2.htm

Strobel, J., & van Barneveld, A. (2009). When is PBL more effective? A meta-synthesis of meta-analyses comparing PBL to conventional classrooms. *Interdisciplinary Journal of Problem-Based Learning, 3*(1), 44–58.

Study Guides and Strategies. (n.d.). *Problem-based learning.* Retrieved from http://www.studygs.net/pbl.htm

Technology for Learning Consortium. (n.d.). *Problem-based learning resources.* Retrieved from http://www.techforlearning.org/PBLresources.html

University of Delaware. (2005). *Problem-based learning at the University of Delaware.* Retrieved from http://www.udel.edu/pbl/problems/

Williamson, V. M., & Rowe, M. W. (2002). Group problem-solving versus lecture in college-level quantitative analysis: The good, the bad, and the ugly. *Journal of Chemical Education, 79*(9), 1131–1134.

Workshop 5.2

Brown, P. (2010, September). Process-oriented guided-inquiry learning in an introductory anatomy and physiology course with a diverse student population. *Advances in Physiology Education, 34,* 150–155.

Eberlein, T., Kampmeier, J., Minderhout, V., Moog, R. S., Platt, T., Varma-Nelson, P., & White, H. B. (2008). Pedagogies of engagement in science: A comparison of PBL, POGIL, and PLTL. *Biochemistry and Molecular Biology Education, 36,* 262–273.

Farrell, J. J., Moog, R. S., & Spencer, J. N. (1999). A guided inquiry general chemistry course. *Journal of Chemical Education, 76*(4), 570–574. doi:10.1021/ed076p570

Hale, D., & Mullen, L. G. (2009). Designing process-oriented guided-inquiry activities: A new innovation for marketing class. *Marketing Education Review, 19,* 73–80.

Hanson, D. M. (2006). *Instructor's guide to process-oriented guided-inquiry learning.* Lisle, IL: Pacific Crest. Retrieved from http://pogil.org/resources/implementation/instructors-guide

Hanson, D. M., & Moog, R. S. (n.d.). *Introduction to POGIL.* Retrieved from http://www.pcrest.com/PC/pub/POGIL.htm

Hanson, D. M., & Wolfskill, T. (2000). Process workshops—A new model for instruction. *Journal of Chemical Education, 77*(1), 120–130. doi:10.1021/ed077p120

Lewis, J. E., & Lewis, S. E. (2005). Departing from lectures: An evaluation of a peer-led guided inquiry alternative. *Journal of Chemical Education, 82*(1), 135–139. doi:10.1021/ed082p135

Moog, R. S., Creegan, F. J., Hanson, D. M., Spencer, J. N., Straumanis, A., Bunce, D. M., & Wolfskill, T. (2009). POGIL: Process-oriented guided-inquiry learning. In N. J. Pienta, M. M. Cooper, & T. J. Greenbowe (Eds.), *Chemists' guide to effective teaching* (Vol. 2, pp. 90–107). Upper Saddle River, NJ: Prentice Hall.

POGIL Project. (2013). Retrieved from http://www.pogil.org/

Straumanis, A., & Simons, E. A. (2008). A multi-institutional assessment of the use of POGIL in organic chemistry. In R. S. Moog & J. N. Spencer (Eds.), *Process-oriented guided inquiry learning* (pp. 224–237). New York, NY: Oxford University Press.

Chapter 3

Principle 6

Anderson, L., & Krathwohl, D. (Ed.). (2001). *A taxonomy for learning, teaching, and assessing: A revision of Bloom's Taxonomy of Educational Objectives* (Complete ed.). New York, NY: Longman.

Andrade, H., & Du, Y. (2007). Student responses to criteria-referenced self-assessment. *Assessment and Evaluation in Higher Education, 32*(2), 159–181. Summarized in *Teaching Professor, 23*, 1.

Angelo, T., & Cross, P. (1993). *Classroom assessment techniques: A handbook for faculty* (2nd ed.). San Francisco, CA: Jossey-Bass.

Black, P., Harrison, C., Lee, C., Marshall, B., & William, D. (2003). *Assessment for learning: Putting it into practice.* Buckingham, UK: Open University Press. Retrieved from http://www.canterbury.ac.uk/education/protected/ppss/docs/gtc-afl.pdf

Black, P., Harrison, C., Lee, C., Marshall, B., & William, D. (2004). Working inside the black box: Assessment for learning in the classroom. *Phi Delta Kappan, 86,* 1–8.

Bloom, B. (1956). *Taxonomy of educational objectives: The classification of educational goals, by a committee of college and university examiners: Handbook 1. Cognitive domain.* New York, NY: Longmans.

Boud, D., Cohen, R., & Sampson, J. (1999). Peer learning assessment. *Assessment and Evaluation in Higher Education, 24*(4), 413–426.

Brookfield, S. D. (1995). *Becoming a critically reflective teacher.* San Francisco, CA: Jossey-Bass.

Brookfield, S. D. (2013). Critical incident questionnaire. Retrieved from http://stephenbrookfield.com/Dr._Stephen_D._Brookfield/Critical_Incident_Questionnaire.html

Butler, A., & Roediger, H. (2008). Feedback enhances the positive effects and reduces the negative effects of multiple-choice testing. *Memory and Cognition, 36*(3), 604–616. Retrieved from http://commonsenseatheism.com/wp-content/uploads/2011/01/Butler-Feedback-enhances-the-positive-effects.pdf

Carpenter, S., Pashler, H., & Cepeda, N. (2009). Using tests to enhance 8th grade students' retention of U.S. history facts. *Applied Cognitive Psychology, 23,* 760–771.

Cauley, K., & McMillan, J. (2010). Formative assessment techniques to support student motivation and achievement. *Clearing House, 83*(1), 1–6.

Cornell University, Center for Teaching Excellence. (2013). What do students already know? Retrieved from http://www.cte.cornell.edu/teaching-ideas/assessing-student-learning/what-do-students-already-know.html

Dietz-Uhler, B., & Lanter, J. R. (2009). Using the four-questions technique to enhance learning. *Teaching of Psychology, 36*(1), 38–41.

Dunlosky, J., Rawson, K., Marsh, E., Nathan, M., & Willingham, D. (2013). Improving students' learning with effective learning techniques: Promising directions from cognitive and educational psychology. *Psychological Science in the Public Interest, 14*(1), 4–58. doi:10.1177/1529100612453266

Educational Origami. (n.d.). Bloom's digital taxonomy. Retrieved from http://edori-gami.wikispaces.com/Bloom%27s+Digital+Taxonomy

Fisher, P., Zeligman, D., & Fairweather, J. (2005). Self-assessed student learning outcomes in an engineering service course. *International Journal of Engineering Education, 21*, 446–456.

Gier, V. S., & Kriener, D. S. (2009). Incorporating active learning with Power-Point–based lectures using content-based questions. *Teaching of Psychology, 36*(2), 134–139.

Greenstein, L. (2010). *What teachers really need to know about formative assessment.* Alexandria, VA: Association for Supervision and Curriculum Development.

Hargreaves, D. (2005). *About learning: Report of the Learning Working Group.* Retrieved from Demos website: http://www.demos.co.uk/publications/about-learning

Higgins, R., Hartley, P., & Skelton, P. (2002). The conscientious consumer: Recon-sidering the role of assessment feedback in student learning. *Studies in Higher Education, 27*(1), 53–64.

Hill, J., & Flynn, K. (2006). *Classroom instruction that works with English language learners.* Alexandria, VA: Association for Supervision and Curricular Develop-ment.

Iowa State University, Center for Learning and Teaching. (2011). A model of learn-ing objectives. Retrieved from http://www.celt.iastate.edu/teaching/Revised-Blooms1.html

Karpicke, J., & Blunt, J. (2011). Retrieval practice produces more learning than elaborative studying with concept mapping. *Science, 331*(6018), 772–775. doi:10.1126/science.1199327

Karpicke, J., & Roediger, H. (2007). Repeated retrieval during learning is the key to long-term retention. *Journal of Memory and Language, 57*, 151–162.

Lord, T., & Baviskar, S. (2007). Moving students from information recitation to information understanding: Exploiting Bloom's taxonomy in creating science questions. *Journal of College Science Teaching, 36*(5), 40–44. Retrieved from http://www.eos.ubc.ca/research/cwsei/resources/Lord%26Baviskar-Blooms.pdf

Lyle, K. B., & Crawford, N. A. (2011). Retrieving essential material at the end of lectures improves performance on statistics exams. *Teaching of Psychology, 38*(2), 94–97.

Mazur, E. (1997). *Peer instruction: A user's manual.* Upper Saddle River, NJ: Prentice Hall.

McConnell, D. (2012). ConcepTests. Retrieved from Carleton College Science Edu-cation Resource Center website: http://serc.carleton.edu/introgeo/conceptests/index.html

McDaniel, M. A., Howard, D. C., & Einstein, G. O. (2009). The read-recite-review study strategy: Effective and portable. *Psychological Science, 20*(4), 516–522.

McDaniel, M. A., Wildman, K. M., & Anderson, J. L. (2012). Using quizzes to enhance summative-assessment performance in a web-based class: An experimental study. *Journal of Applied Research in Memory and Cognition, 1*, 18–26.

McKeachie, W., & Svinicki, M. (2013). *McKeachie's teaching tips: Strategies, research, and theory for college and university teachers* (14th ed.). Belmont, CA: Wadsworth.

McTighe, J., & Emberger, M. (2006). Teamwork on assessments creates powerful professional development. *Journal of Staff Development, 27*(1), 38–44.

Morton, J. P. (2007, June). The active review: One final task to end the lecture. *Advances in Physiology Education, 31*, 236–237.

Nilson, L. B. (2010). *Teaching at its best: A research-based resource for college instructors* (3rd ed., pp. 273–294). San Francisco, CA: Jossey-Bass.

Novak, G., Patterson, E., Gavrin, A., Christian, W., & Forinash, K. (1999). Just in Time Teaching. *American Journal of Physics, 67*(10), 937. doi:10.1119/1.19159

Pyc, M. A., & Rawson, K. A. (2010). Why testing improves memory: Mediator effectiveness hypothesis. *Science, 330*(6002), 335. *doi:*10.1126/science.1191465

Roediger, H. L., Agarwal, P. K., McDaniel, M. A., & McDermott, K. B. (2011). Test-enhanced learning in the classroom: Long-term benefits from quizzing. *Journal of Experimental Psychology: Applied, 17*(4), 382–395. doi:10.1037/a0026252

Roediger, H., & Karpicke, J. D. (2006). Test-enhanced learning: Taking memory tests improves long-term retention. *Psychological Science, 17*(3), 249–255.

Rohrer, D. (2009). The effects of spacing and mixing practice problems. *Journal for Research in Mathematics Education, 40*, 4–17.

Rohrer, D., & Taylor, K. (2006). The effects of overlearning and distributed practice on the retention of mathematics knowledge. *Applied Cognitive Psychology, 20*, 1209–1224.

Shepard, L. A. (2005). *Formative assessment: Caveat emptor.* Retrieved from http://www.cpre.org/ccii/images/stories/ccii_pdfs/shepard%20formative%20assessment%20caveat%20emptor.pdf

Stake, R. (2004). *Standards-based and responsive evaluation.* Thousand Oaks, CA: Sage Publications.

University of Illinois Online Network. (n.d.). Online teaching activity index: KWL. Retrieved from http://www.ion.uillinois.edu/resources/otai/KWL.asp

University of Massachusetts–Amherst, Office of Academic Planning and Assessment. (n.d.). *Course-based review and assessment methods for understanding student learning.* Retrieved from http://www.umass.edu/oapa/oapa/publications/online_handbooks/course_based.pdf

University of North Carolina–Charlotte, Center for Teaching and Learning. (2004). Writing objectives using Bloom's taxonomy. Retrieved from http://teaching.uncc.edu/articles-books/best-practice-articles/goals-objectives/writing-objectives-using-blooms-taxonomy

Vanderbilt University, Center for Teaching. (n.d.). Classroom assessment techniques. Retrieved from http://cft.vanderbilt.edu/teaching-guides/assessment/cats/

Zull, J. E. (2002). *The art of changing the brain: Enriching the practice of teaching by exploring the biology of learning* (pp. 203–220). Sterling, VA: Stylus.

Workshop 6.1

Bailey, R., & Garner, M. (2010). Is the feedback in higher education assessment worth the paper it is written on? Teachers' reflections on their practices. *Teaching in Higher Education, 15*(2), 187–198.

Bean, J. C. (2011). *Engaging ideas: The professor's guide to integrating writing, critical thinking, and active learning in the classroom* (2nd ed., pp. 267–289). San Francisco, CA: Jossey-Bass.

Bean, J. C., & Peterson, D. (1998). Grading classroom participation. *New directions for teaching and learning, 74*, 33–40.

Bloom, B. (1956). *Taxonomy of educational objectives: The classification of educational goals, by a committee of college and university examiners: Handbook 1. Cognitive domain.* New York, NY: Longmans.

Brigham Young University, Faculty Center. (2001). 14 rules for writing multiple-choice questions. Retrieved from http://testing.byu.edu/info/handbooks/14%20 Rules%20for%20Writing%20Multiple-Choice%20Questions.pdf

Brown, E., & Glover, C. (2006). Evaluating written feedback. In C. Bryan & K. Clegg (Eds.), *Innovative assessment in higher education* (pp. 81–91). New York, NY: Routledge.

Bruner, J. (1961). The act of discovery. *Harvard Educational Review, 31*, 21–32.

Burke, D. (2009). Strategies for using feedback students bring to higher education. *Assessment and Evaluation in Higher Education, 34*(1), 41–50.

Burton, S. J., Sudweeks, R. R., Merrill, P. F., & Wood, B. (1991). *How to prepare better multiple-choice test items: Guidelines for university faculty.* Retrieved from Brigham Young University Testing Center website: http://testing.byu.edu/info/ handbooks/betteritems.pdf

Carless, D. (2006). Differing perceptions in the feedback process. *Studies in Higher Education, 31*(2), 219–233.

Coleman, L. (2002). *Grading student papers: Some guidelines for commenting on and grading students' written work in any discipline.* Retrieved from University of Maryland Center for Teaching Excellence website: http://www.cte.umd.edu/ teaching/resources/GradingHandbook.pdf

Cornell University, Center for Teaching Excellence. (n.d.). Course-level assessment methods. Retrieved from http://www.cte.cornell.edu/teaching-ideas/assessing-student-learning/course-level-assessment-guide.html#assessmentmethods

Crisp, B. R. (2007). Is it worth the effort? How feedback influences students' subsequent submission of assessable work. *Assessment and Evaluation in Higher Education, 32*(5), 571–581.

Myers, C. B., & Myers, S. M. (2007). Assessing assessments: The effects of two exam formats on course achievement and evaluation. *Innovative Higher Education, 31*, 227–236.

Nilson, L. B. (2010). *Teaching at its best: A research-based resource for college instructors* (3rd ed., pp. 273–280). San Francisco, CA: Jossey-Bass.

Rowntree, D. (1987). *Assessing students: How shall we know them?* New York, NY: Taylor & Francis.

Schechter, E. (Ed.). (2011). *Internet resources for higher education outcomes assessment.* Retrieved from http://www2.acs.ncsu.edu/UPA/archives/assmt/resource.htm

Suskie, L. (2009). *Assessing student learning: A commonsense guide* (2nd ed.). Bolton, MA: Anker.

Vanderbilt University, Center for Teaching. (n.d.). Classroom assessment techniques. Retrieved from http://cft.vanderbilt.edu/teaching-guides/assessment/cats/

Vanderbilt University, Center for Teaching. (n.d.) Writing good multiple choice test questions. Retrieved from http://cft.vanderbilt.edu/teaching-guides/assessment/writing-good-multiple-choice-test-questions/

Wiggins, G., & McTighe, J. (2005). *Understanding by design* (pp. 146–171). Alexandria, VA: Association for Supervision and Curricular Development.

Workshop 6.1A

Bloom, B. (1956). *Taxonomy of educational objectives: The classification of educational goals, by a committee of college and university examiners: Handbook 1. Cognitive domain.* New York, NY: Longmans.

Brigham Young University, Faculty Center. (2001). 14 rules for writing multiple-choice questions. Retrieved from http://testing.byu.edu/info/handbooks/14%20Rules%20for%20Writing%20Multiple-Choice%20Questions.pdf

Bruff, D. (2009–2010). Multiple-choice questions you wouldn't put on a test: Promoting deep learning using clickers. *Essays on Teaching Excellence, 21*(3). Retrieved from http://podnetwork.org/content/uploads/V21-N3-Bruff.pdf

Burton, S. J., Sudweeks, R. R., Merrill, P. F., & Wood, B. (1991). *How to prepare better multiple-choice test items: Guidelines for university faculty.* Retrieved from Brigham Young University Testing Center website: http://testing.byu.edu/info/handbooks/betteritems.pdf

Harvard University, Derek Bok Center for Teaching and Learning. (2006). Grading papers. Retrieved from http://isites.harvard.edu/fs/html/icb.topic58474/GradingPapers.html

Jacobs, L. (n.d.). *How to write better tests: A handbook for improving test construction skills.* Retrieved from Indiana University–Bloomington website: http://www.indiana.edu/~best/pdf_docs/better_tests.pdf

Reiner, C., Bothell, T., Sudweeks, R., & Wood, B. (2002). *Preparing effective essay questions: A self-directed workbook for educators.* Stillwater, OK: New Forums Press. Retrieved from *Brigham Young University Testing Center website:* http://testing.byu.edu/info/handbooks/WritingEffectiveEssayQuestions.pdf

Teaching Effectiveness Program. (2013, May 16). Writing multiple-choice questions that demand critical thinking. Retrieved from University of Oregon Teaching and Learning Center website: http://tep.uoregon.edu/resources/assessment/multiplechoicequestions/mc4critthink.html

University of Washington, Center for Teaching and Learning. (n.d.). Constructing tests: Essay questions. Retrieved from http://www.washington.edu/teaching/constructing-tests/#essayquestions

Vanderbilt University, Center for Teaching. (n.d.). Grading student work. Retrieved from http://cft.vanderbilt.edu/teaching-guides/assessment/grading-student-work/

Vanderbilt University, Center for Teaching. (n.d.). Writing good multiple choice test questions. Retrieved from http://cft.vanderbilt.edu/teaching-guides/assessment/writing-good-multiple-choice-test-questions/

Workshop 6.1B

Kappa Omicron Nu Honor Society. (2013). Rubric samples for higher education. Retrieved from http://rubrics.kappaomicronnu.org/contact.html

Mitstifer, D. (2013). Undergraduate research paper rubric. Retrieved from Kappa Omicron Nu Honor Society website: http://rubrics.kappaomicronnu.org/rubric-documents/Undergraduate-Research-Paper-Rubric4.pdf

Mueller, J. F. (2012). *Authentic assessment toolbox.* Retrieved from http://jfmueller.faculty.noctrl.edu/toolbox/rubrics.htm

Pickett, N. (1999). Guidelines for rubric development. Retrieved from http://edweb.sdsu.edu/triton/july/rubrics/rubric_guidelines.html

Stevens, D. (2004). *Introduction to rubrics: An assessment tool to save grading time, convey effective feedback, and promote student learning.* Sterling, VA: Stylus.

Stevens, D., & Levi, A. (2013). *Introduction to rubrics: An assessment tool to save grading time, convey effective feedback and promote student learning* (2nd ed.). Sterling, VA: Stylus.

University of Colorado–Denver, Center for Faculty Development. (2006). Creating a rubric. Retrieved from http://www.ucdenver.edu/faculty_staff/faculty/center-for-faculty-development/Documents/Tutorials/Rubrics/index.htm

University of Massachusetts–Amherst, Office of Academic Planning and Assessment. (n.d.) *Course-based review and assessment methods for understanding student learning.* Retrieved from http://www.umass.edu/oapa/oapa/publications/online_handbooks/course_based.pdf

Wiggins, G., & McTighe, J. (2005). *Understanding by design* (pp. 146–171). Alexandria, VA: Association for Supervision and Curricular Development.

Workshop 6.1C

Harvard University, Derek Bok Center for Teaching and Learning. (2006). Grading papers. Retrieved from http://isites.harvard.edu/fs/html/icb.topic58474/GradingPapers.html

Orsmond, P., Merry, S., & Reitch, K. (1996). The importance of marking criteria in the use of peer assessment. *Assessment and Evaluation in Higher Education, 21*(3), 239–249.

Rae, A., & Cochrane, D. (2008). Listening to students: How to make written assessment feedback useful. *Active Learning in Higher Education, 9*(3), 217–230.

Ruszkiewicz, R. (2009). *How to write anything: A guide and reference.* New York, NY: Bedford/St. Martin.

Semke, H. D. (1984). Effects of the red pen. *Foreign Language Annals, 17*(3), 195–202. Retrieved from http://www.annenbergmedia.org/workshops/tfl/resources/s3_redpen.pdf

Shaw, H. (1984). Responding to student essays. In F. V. Bogel & K. Gottschalk (Eds.), *Teaching prose: A guide for writing instructors.* New York, NY: Norton. Retrieved from https://my.hamilton.edu/writing/writing-resources/how-i-assign-letter-grades

Vanderbilt University, Center for Teaching. (n.d.). Grading student work. Retrieved from http://cft.vanderbilt.edu/teaching-guides/assessment/grading-student-work/

Walvoord, B., & Anderson, V. (1998). *Effective grading* (pp. 128–129). San Francisco, CA: Jossey-Bass.

Walvoord, B., & Banta, T. (2010). *Assessment clear and simple: A practical guide for institutions, departments, and general education.* San Francisco, CA: Jossey-Bass.

Workshop 6.2

Brigham Young University, Center for Teaching and Learning. (n.d.). Using mid-course evaluations. Retrieved from http://ctl.byu.edu/collections/using-mid-course-evaluations

Clark, D. J., & Redmond, M. (1982). *Small group instructional diagnosis: Final report.* Available from ERIC Document Reproduction Service. (No. ED217954)

Coconino Community College. (2010). *Mid-course evaluations.* Retrieved from http://www.coconino.edu/research/Pages/MidCourseEvaluations.aspx

Cohen, P. (1980). Effectiveness of student-rating feedback for improving college instruction: A meta-analysis of findings. *Research in Higher Education, 13*(4), 321–341.

Cook-Sather, A. (2009). From traditional accountability to shared responsibility: The benefits and challenges of student consultants gathering midcourse feedback in college classrooms. *Assessment and Evaluation in Higher Education, 34*(2), 231–241.

Croxall, B. (2012, February 21). Conducting your midterm evaluations publicly with Google docs [web log post]. *ProfHacker.* Retrieved from http://chronicle.com/blogs/profhacker/make-your-midterm-evaluations-public-with-google-docs/38680

Diamond, R. (2004). The usefulness of structured mid-term feedback as a catalyst for change in higher education classes. *Active Learning in Higher Education, 5*(3), 217–231.

Lewis, K. G. (2001). Using midsemester student feedback and responding to it. *New Directions in Teaching and Learning, 87,* 33–44.

Millis, B., & Vazquez, M. (2010). Quick course diagnosis (QCD) and the structured focus groups. Retrieved from California State University–Channel Islands website: http://facultydevelopment.csuci.edu/on_line_resources.htm

Millis, B., & Vazquez, J. (2010–2011). Down with the SGID! Long live the QCD! *Essays on Teaching Excellence, 22*(4). Retrieved from http://podnetwork.org/content/uploads/V22_N4_Millis_Vasquez.pdf

Nilson, L. B. (2010). *Teaching at its best: A research-based resource for college instructors* (3rd ed., pp. 315–328). San Francisco, CA: Jossey-Bass.

Sorenson, D. L. (2001). College teachers and student consultants: Collaborating about teaching and learning. In D. Miller, J. Groccia, & M. Miller (Eds.), *Student-assisted teaching: A guide to faculty-student teamwork* (pp. 228–239). San Francisco, CA: Jossey-Bass.

Appendix A

Workshop A.1

Bain, K. (2004). *What the best college teachers do* (pp. 48–67). Cambridge, MA: Harvard University Press.

Bowen, J. (2012). *Teaching naked: How moving technology out of your college classroom will improve student learning.* San Francisco, CA: Jossey-Bass.

Concepción, D. W. (2009–2010). Transparent alignment and integrated course design. *Essays on Teaching Excellence, 21*(2). Retrieved from http://podnetwork.org/content/uploads/V21-N2-Concepcion.pdf

Diamond, R. (2008). *Designing and assessing courses and curricula* (3rd ed.). San Francisco, CA: Jossey-Bass.

Fink, L. D. (2005, August). *A self-directed guide to designing courses for significant learning.* Retrieved from http://www.deefinkandassociates.com/GuidetoCourseDesignAug05.pdf

Fink, L. D. (2013). *Creating significant learning experiences: An integrated approach to designing college courses* (Rev. ed.). San Francisco, CA: Jossey-Bass.

Groom, W. (1994). Gumpisms: The wit and wisdom of Forrest Gump. New York, NY: Pocket Books.

Harnish, R., McElwee, R., Slattery, J., Frantz, S., Haney, M., Shore, C., & Penley, J. (2011). Creating the foundation for a warm classroom climate: Best practices in syllabus tone. *Observer, 24*(1). Retrieved from http://www.psychologicalscience.org/index.php/publications/observer/2011/january-11/creating-the-foundation-for-a-warm-classroom-climate.html

Hara, B. (2010, October 19). Graphic display of student learning objectives [web log post]. *ProfHacker.* Retrieved from http://chronicle.com/blogs/profhacker/graphic-display-of-student-learning-objectives/27863

Huxham, M. (2005). Learning in lectures: Do "interactive windows" help? *Active Learning in Higher Education, 6*(1), 17–31.

Lattuca, L., & Stark, J. (2009). *Shaping the college curriculum: Academic plans in context.* Hoboken, NJ: Wiley & Sons.

Lowther, M. A., Stark, J. S., & Martens, G. G. (1989). *Preparing course syllabi for improved communication*. Washington DC: Office of Educational Research and Improvement.

Nilson, L. B. (2007). *The graphic syllabus and the outcomes map: Communicating your course*. San Francisco, CA: Jossey-Bass.

Nilson, L. B. (2010). *Teaching at its best: A research-based resource for college instructors* (3rd ed., pp. 33–37). San Francisco, CA: Jossey-Bass.

O'Brien, J. G., Millis, B. J., & Cohen, M. W. (2008). *The course syllabus: A learning centered approach* (2nd ed.). San Francisco, CA: Jossey-Bass.

Singham, M. (2007). Death to the syllabus! *Liberal Education, 93*(4), 52–56. Retrieved from http://www.aacu.org/liberaleducation/le-fa07/le_fa07_myview.cfm

Slattery, J. M., & Carlson, J. (2005). Preparing an effective syllabus: Current best practices. *College Teaching, 53*(4), 159–164.

Terry, W. (2005). Serial position effects in recall of television commercials. *Journal of General Psychology, 132*(2), 151–163.

University of Minnesota, Center for Teaching and Learning. (2008). Student roles. Retrieved from http://www1.umn.edu/ohr/teachlearn/tutorials/syllabus/expectations/student/index.html

Wasley, P. (2008a). Research yields tips on crafting better syllabi. *Chronicle of Higher Education, 54*(27), A11–A12.

Wasley, P. (2008b). The syllabus becomes a repository of legalese. *Chronicle of Higher Education, 54*(27), A1–A10.

Wiggins, G., & McTighe, J. (2005). *Understanding by design* (pp. 13–34). Alexandria, VA: Association for Supervision and Curricular Development.

Workshop A.2

Ambrose, S. A., Bridges, M. W., DiPietro, M., Lovett, M. C., & Norman, M. K. (2010). *How learning works: Seven research-based principles for smart teaching* (p. 84). San Francisco, CA: Jossey-Bass.

Bennett, K. L. (2004). How to start teaching a tough course: Dry organization versus excitement on the first day of class. *College Teaching, 52*(3), 106.

Bowen, J. (2012). *Teaching naked: How moving technology out of your college classroom will improve student learning*. San Francisco, CA: Jossey-Bass.

Carnegie Mellon University, Eberly Center. (n.d.). Make the most of the first day of class. Retrieved from http://www.cmu.edu/teaching/designteach/teach/firstday.html

Cox, K. J. (2005). Group introductions—Get-acquainted team building activity. Retrieved from http://www.docstoc.com/docs/34260610/Group-Introductions-Get-Acquainted-Team-Building

Douglas, C. (2013). Wrap-up activities for training professionals. Retrieved from Leadership Strategies website: http://www.leadstrat.com/component/content/article/12-forfacilitators/122-wrap-up-activities-for-training-professionals

Fleming, N. (2003). *Establishing rapport: Personal interaction and learning* (IDEA Paper No. 39). Retrieved from Idea Center website: http://www.theideacenter.org/sites/default/files/IDEA_Paper_39.pdf

Goza, B. K. (1993). Graffiti needs assessment: Involving students in the first class session. *Journal of Management Education, 17*(1), 99–106.

Grimes, J., & Desrochers, C. (2010). Making your first class session really first class [Video]. Retrieved from http://elixr.merlot.org/case-stories/course-preparation--design/first-day-of-class/goals-for-first-day-of-class7

Harnish, R., McElwee R., Slattery, J., Frantz, S., Haney, M., Shore, C., & Penley, J. (2011). Creating the foundation for a warm classroom climate: Best practices in syllabus tone. *Observer, 24*(1). Retrieved from http://www.psychologicalscience .org/index.php/publications/observer/2011/january-11/creating-the-foundation-for-a-warm-classroom-climate.html

Iowa State University, Center for Excellence in Teaching and Learning. (2011). Welcoming students on the first day [Video]. Retrieved from http://www.celt.iastate .edu/teaching/video/welcoming.html

Lang, J. M. (2006). Finishing strong. *Chronicle of Higher Education, 53*(9), C2. Retrieved from http://chronicle.com/article/Finishing-Strong/46812/

Lyons, R., McIntosh, M., & Kysilka, M. (2003). *Teaching college in an age of accountability* (p. 87). Boston, MA: Allyn and Bacon.

Maier, M. H., & Panitz, T. (1996). Ending on a high note: Better endings for classes and courses. Retrieved from http://home.capecod.net/~tpanitz/tedsarticles/endingcourses.htm

Nilson, L. B. (2010). *Teaching at its best: A research-based resource for college instructors* (3rd ed., pp. 26–27). San Francisco, CA: Jossey-Bass.

Palmer, M. (n.d.). Not quite 101 ways to learning students' names. Retrieved from University of Virginia Teaching Resource Center website: http://trc.virginia.edu/ teaching-tips/not-quite-101-ways-to-learning-students-names/

Pascarella, E. T., & Terenzini, P. T. (2005). *How college affects students.* San Francisco, CA: Jossey-Bass.

Provitera McGlynn, A. (2001). *Successful beginnings for college teaching: Engaging students from the first day.* Madison, WI: Atwood.

Uhl, C. (2005). The last class. *College Teaching, 53*(4), 165–166.

Weimer, M. (2013, January 9). First day of class activities that create a climate for learning [web log post]. *Teaching Professor Blog.* Retrieved from http://www .facultyfocus.com/articles/teaching-professor-blog/first-day-of-class-activities-that-create-a-climate-for-learning/

Appendix B

Workshop B.1

Bask, K., & Bailey, E. (2002). Are faculty role models? *Journal of Economic Education, 33*(2), 99–124.

Bligh, D. A. (2000). *What's the use of lectures?* San Francisco, CA: Jossey-Bass.

Bodie, G., Powers, W., & Fitch-Hauser, M. (2006, August). Chunking, priming and active learning: Toward an innovative and blended approach to teaching communication-related skills. *Interactive Learning Environments, 14*(2), 119–135.

Burns, R. A. (1985, May). *Information impact and factors affecting recall.* Paper presented at the Annual National Conference on Teaching Excellence and Conference of Administrators, Austin, TX. Available from ERIC Document Reproduction Service. (No. ED258639)

Davis, D. (2008). A brain-friendly environment for learning. Retrieved from Faculty Focus website: http://www.facultyfocus.com/articles/instructional-design/a-brain-friendly-environment-for-learning/

Denman, M. (2005). How to create memorable lectures. *Speaking of Teaching, 14*(1), 1–5. Retrieved from http://www.stanford.edu/dept/CTL/Newsletter/memorable_lectures.pdf

Drummond, T. (1995). A brief summary of the best practices in college teaching. Retrieved from University of North Carolina–Charlotte Center for Teaching and Learning website: http://teaching.uncc.edu/articles-books/best-practice-articles/course-development/best-practices

Graesser, A. C., Olde, B., & Klettke, B. (2002). How does the mind construct and represent stories? In M. C. Green, J. J. Strange, & T. C. Brock (Eds.), *Narrative impact: Social and cognitive foundations* (pp. 231–263). Mahwah, NJ: Lawrence Erlbaum Associates.

Halpern, D., & Hakel, M. (2003). Applying the science of learning. *Change, 35*(4), 36–41.

Hamm, P. H. (2006). *Teaching and persuasive communication: Class presentation skills.* Retrieved from Brown University Harriet W. Sheridan Center for Teaching and Learning website: http://brown.edu/about/administration/sheridan-center/sites/brown.edu.about.administration.sheridan-center/files/uploads/Teaching%20and%20Persuasive%20Communication.pdf

Heath, C., & Heath, D. (2010). *Teaching that sticks.* Retrieved from http://groups.haas.berkeley.edu/CTE/documents/Teaching%20That%20Sticks.pdf

Hoyt, D., & Perera, S. (2000). *Teaching approach, instructional objectives, and learning* (IDEA Research Report No. 1). Retrieved from Idea Center website: http://www.theideacenter.org/sites/default/files/research1.pdf

Huxham, M. (2005). Learning in lectures: Do "interactive windows" help? *Active Learning in Higher Education, 6*(1), 17–31.

Karpicke, J., & Blunt, J. (2011). Retrieval practice produces more learning than elaborative studying with concept mapping. *Science, 331*(6018), 772–775. doi:10.1126/science.1199327

King, A. (1993). From sage on the stage to guide on the side. *College Teaching, 41*(1), 30–35.

McKeachie, W. J., & Svinicki, M. (2013). *Teaching tips: Strategies, research, and theory for college and university teachers* (14th ed.). Belmont, CA: Wadsworth.

Medina, J. (2008). *Brain rules* (pp. 73–93). Seattle, WA: Pear Press.

Nilson, L. B. (2010). *Teaching at its best: A research-based resource for college instructors* (3rd ed., pp. 113–125). San Francisco, CA: Jossey-Bass.

Reed, S. K. (2006). *Cognition: Theory and applications* (7th ed). Belmont, CA: Wadsworth.

Roediger, H., & Karpicke, J. (2006). Test-enhanced learning taking memory tests improves long-term retention. *Psychological Science, 17*(3), 249–255.

Ruhl, K. L., Hughes, C. A., & Schloss, P. J. (1987). Using the pause procedure to enhance lecture recall. *Teacher Education and Special Education, 10,* 14.

Terry, W. (2005). Serial position effects in recall of television commercials. *Journal of General Psychology, 132*(2), 151–163.

University of California–Berkeley, Center for Teaching and Learning. (n.d.). Large lecture classes: Six ways to make lectures in a large enrollment course more manageable and effective. Retrieved from http://teaching.berkeley.edu/large-lecture-classes

University of Minnesota, Center for Teaching and Learning. (2010). Planning lectures. Retrieved from http://www1.umn.edu/ohr/teachlearn/tutorials/lectures/planning/index.html

Wald, G. (1969). A generation in search of a future [Lecture]. Retrieved from http://www.elijahwald.com/generation.html

Appendix C

Workshop C.1

Bain, K. (2004). *What the best college teachers do* (pp. 48–67). Cambridge, MA: Harvard University Press.

Baxter, J., & Bush, R. T. (2010). Classroom discussion as a skill, not a technique. Retrieved from DePaul University Teaching Commons website: http://teaching-commons.depaul.edu/Classroom_Activities/discussion.html

Brookfield, S. (2006). *The skillful teacher* (pp. 115–131). San Francisco, CA: Jossey-Bass.

Brookfield, S., & Preskill, S. (2005). *Discussion as a way of teaching: Tools and techniques for democratic classrooms.* San Francisco, CA: Jossey-Bass.

Dawes, J. (2007). Ten strategies for effective discussion leading. Retrieved from Harvard University Derek Bok Center for Teaching and Learning website: http://isites.harvard.edu/fs/html/icb.topic58474/Dawes_DL.html

Duquesne University, Center for Teaching Excellence. (2004). *Facilitating classroom discussions.* Retrieved from http://www.duq.edu/Documents/cte/_pdf/classroom-discussions.pdf

Frederick, P. (1981). The dreaded discussion: Ten ways to start. *Improving College and University Teaching, 29*(3), 109–114. Retrieved from http://www.indiana.edu/~tchsotl/part%201/part1%20materials/The_Dreaded_Discussion.pdf

Henning, J. E. (2005). Leading discussions: Opening up the conversation. *College Teaching, 53*(3), 90–95.

hooks, b. (1994). *Teaching to transgress: Education as the practice of freedom.* New York, NY: Routledge.

Huston, T. (2009). *Teaching what you don't know* (pp. 144–165). Cambridge, MA: Harvard University Press.

Looking at Student Work. (n.d.) Protocols. Retrieved from http://www.lasw.org/protocols.html

McDonald, J. P., Mohr, N., Dichter, A., & McDonald, E. C. (2007). *The power of protocols: An educator's guide to better practice* (2nd ed.). New York, NY: Teacher's College Press.

McDonald, J. P., Zydney, J. M., Dichter, A., & McDonald, E. C. (2012). Abbreviated protocols. Retrieved from Teachers College Press website: http://www.tcpress.com/pdfs/mcdonaldprot.pdf

Nilson, L. B. (2010). *Teaching at its best: A research-based resource for college instructors* (3rd ed., pp. 113–125). San Francisco, CA: Jossey-Bass.

Nunn, C. E. (1996). Discussion in the college classroom: Triangulating observational and survey results. *Journal of Higher Education, 67*(3), 243–266.

Pennsylvania State University, Schreyer Institute for Teaching Excellence. (2013). Using discussion in the classroom. Retrieved from http://www.schreyerinstitute.psu.edu/tools/Discuss/

Ross, W. (1860). Methods of instruction. *Barnard's American Journal of Education, 9,* 367–379.

Rotenberg, R. (2005). The discussion classroom. In R. Rotenberg (Ed.), *The art and craft of college teaching: A guide for new professors and graduate students* (pp. 131–143). Chicago, IL: Active Learning Books.

Smith, M., Wood, W., Adams, W., Wieman, C., Knight J., Guild, N., & Su, T. (2009). Why peer discussion improves student performance on in-class concept questions. *Science, 323*(5910), 122–124.

Stanford University, Center for Teaching and Learning. (2003). The Socratic method: What is it and how to use it in the classroom. *Speaking of Teaching, 13*(1). Retrieved from https://www.stanford.edu/dept/CTL/Newsletter/socratic_method.pdf

INDEX

Idea-Based Learning

A Course Design Process to Promote Conceptual Understanding

Edmund J. Hansen

"*Idea-Based Learning* has much to commend it. It is not directed toward any specific discipline; instead, Hansen has included examples from across the curriculum. Hansen's book is readable and thought-provoking. It does not bog down the reader with excessive theory or debate, but rather seeks to be a concise guidebook for course design. It is an excellent starting point for new teachers, while also offering something to those more seasoned in the classroom. Finally, his work provides enough context that the reader is encouraged to move beyond this particular work in order to gain further depth into one's own reflection on teaching."

—Forrest Clingerman,
Ohio Northern University, in Teaching Theology & Religion

Sty/us

22883 Quicksilver Drive
Sterling, VA 20166-2102   Subscribe to our e-mail alerts: www.Styluspub.com

Also available from Stylus

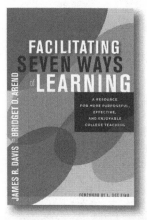

Facilitating Seven Ways of Learning
A Resource for More Purposeful, Effective, and Enjoyable College Teaching
James R. Davis and Bridget D. Arend
Foreword by L. Dee Fink

"In a crowded marketplace of snake oil cure-alls for higher education comes this refreshingly straight-forward, sensible, and practical guide for college teachers. As Davis and Arend point out, learning is not just one thing, but many. Learning a skill is different from learning information, which is different form learning to think critically or creatively. It follows that there cannot be one way to teach it all. With careful attention to the research about multiple types of learning, Davis and Arend have provided a treasure trove of tips and techniques, from low-tech engaging discussions to high-tech virtual reality simulations, to help college teachers create learning environments that work."

—Michael Wesch,
2008 US Professor of the Year, University Distinguished Teaching Scholar, Kansas State University

"Slam dunk, touchdown, goal, grand slam, ace!!! This book is fabulous. Davis and Arend have pulled together an exceptional resource for better understanding effective teaching strategies by demonstrating how to adjust teaching based on what students need to learn. As faculty, we expect students to learn a wide variety of concepts, processes, and applications. To accomplish this, research clearly suggests using a variety of strategies. This book not only explains that research, but also gives concrete examples and a solid rationale for each learning approach.

While the authors note this material is not intended for those brand new to teaching, and although I believe just about anyone teaching at the postsecondary level could learn from this book, the primary audience really is faculty who are looking to rethink what they are currently doing. This book will result in seriously reassessing how to best facilitate learning.

This is the perfect book for groups and reading circles of experienced teachers. I will certainly add to my faculty development collection."

—Todd Zakrajsek,
Associate Professor, School of Medicine, University of North Carolina at Chapel Hill